Bags
- a Knitter's dozen

a production of  BOOKS

Credits

Bags; A Knitter's dozen PUBLISHED BY XRX BOOKS

PUBLISHER
Alexis Yiorgos Xenakis

MANAGING EDITOR
David Xenakis

COEDITORS
Rick Mondragon
Elaine Rowley

EDITORIAL ASSISTANT
Sue Nelson

EDITORIAL INTERN
Jasmin Karimzadeh

INSTRUCTION EDITOR
Joni Coniglio

INSTRUCTION ASSISTANT
Cole Kelley

COPY EDITOR
Holly Brunner

GRAPHIC DESIGNER
Bob Natz

PHOTOGRAPHER
Alexis Xenakis

SECOND PHOTOGRAPHER
Mike Winkleman

PRODUCTION DIRECTOR &
COLOR SPECIALIST
Dennis Pearson

BOOK PRODUCTION
MANAGER
Susan Becker

PRODUCTION
Everett Baker
Nancy Holzer

TECHNICAL ILLUSTRATIONS
Jay Reeve
Carol Skallerud

SPECIAL ILLUSTRATIONS
Natalie Sorenson

MIS
Jason Bittner

SECOND PRINTING 2004
FIRST PUBLISHED IN USA IN 2004 BY XRX, INC.

COPYRIGHT © 2004 XRX, INC.

ISBN 1-893762-20-3

Produced in Sioux Falls, South Dakota, by XRX, Inc.,
PO Box 1525, Sioux Falls, SD 57101-1525 USA 605.338.2450
a publication of XRX **BOOKS**

Visit us online at www.knittinguniverse.com

XRX BOOKS

Bags
- a Knitter's dozen

PHOTOGRAPHY BY ALEXIS XENAKIS

1
Market Squares

2
Flaps

3
Snaps

4
Felted
Pocketbook

5
Three
For the Road

6
SoHo Sling

11
Gallery Bags

12
Zigzag Bags

13
Four-Square
Mitered Tote

14
It's in the Bag

15
Season-Spanners
Duo

16
Fabulous Felted
Backpacks

a Knitter's dozen CONTENTS

Welcome

In my life, the important question is no longer, "Which hat am I wearing today?" but "Which bag (or bags) am I carrying?"

Perhaps this is unique to me: I've always been notorious for toting most parts of my work (and play) with me—just in case. Although a drive will last only an hour, better take along a week's-worth of knitting and a good book or two; you never can tell. This habit may come from living on the Prairie—no matter what the weather, I'm always prepared for the Blizzard of '96 (or whatever year the last big one was)—but it's a life-long pattern, not apt to change.

What has changed is the bag. Once the quest was for the perfect, multi-purpose, all-accommodating carryall. Now my approach is modular—several small bags that can be combined and recombined to allow me to carry as much as, but no more than, a day or a flight or a lunch break requires.

This many-bag approach to multitasking gives me the excuse to have lots of bags. Less, obviously; it helps me focus. When I pick up my littlest knitting bag, I know what I'm going to do (knit) and even better, I know what I'm going to knit (whatever it holds); no need to consider the pros and cons of working on the handful of undones that circle around me at home. There are times when I really appreciate having no choices.

My solution to this one of life's little problems may or may not be yours, but once you start, I wager you may find it equally hard to resist knitting yet another bag. It's so easy to just pick up a couple of skeins of something you love and cast on. Soon your knitter's dozen, like ours, will grow to twenty-something . . . or more.

Elaine Rowley

Throughout this book, the yarns are described generically and the specific yarn is listed with each photograph. Some of the yarns are no longer available, but may live on in our memories and stashes.

Here's our all-time favorite tote bag! Take this felted entrelac tote shopping, on a picnic, or pack it with your current knitting project. Choose the sunny colorway, create your own, or try a rich handpaint.

Designed by Lynda Cyr

Market Squares

INTERMEDIATE+

42" circumference
at widest point, after felting

10cm/4"

21
16
• over stockinette stitch
(knit on RS, purl on WS), before felting

1 2 3 **4** 5 6

• Medium weight
A • 243 yds
B, C, D, E • 162 yds each

• 5mm/US8, or size to obtain gauge,
60 cm (24") long

• Two 5mm/US8 double-pointed needles
(dpn)

Note
See *Techniques*, p. 80, for ssk and SSSK.

BAG
Band
With B, cast on 144 sts. Place marker, join and knit every round for 1".
Join hem as follows:
Next round Fold cast-on edge up in front of sts on needle, then * insert right-hand needle into 1 st from cast-on edge and into first st on left-hand needle, k2tog; repeat from * around, forming a tube. Cut yarn.
Notes 1 Rest of bag is worked in tiers of triangles or rectangles. Odd-numbered tiers are worked from right to left, with sts picked up and knit with RS of work facing (sts of Tier 1 are knit directly from Band); even-numbered tiers are worked from left to right, with sts picked up and purled with WS of work facing. **2** Turn work after every row, unless indicated otherwise. **3** Cut yarn after every tier.

Tier 1
MAKE 12 BASE TRIANGLES WITH C.
Row 1 (RS) K2.
Row 2 and all WS rows Purl to end of triangle being worked.

Row 3 K3.
Row 5 K3, ssk.
Row 7 K5.
Row 9 K6.
Row 11 K6, ssk.
Row 13 K8.
Row 15 K10, do not turn—triangle complete.
Repeat from * 11 times more. Turn work after last triangle has been worked.

Tier 2
MAKE 12 RECTANGLES WITH A.
With WS facing and right-hand needle, pick up and purl 11 sts along Triangle 1 from Tier 1. * Slip last picked-up st to left-hand needle, p2tog (picked-up st together with 1 st of next triangle).
Row 1 and all RS rows Knit.
Rows 2 and 4 Purl to last st of rectangle, p2tog (with 1 st of next triangle).
Row 6 Purl to last st, p3tog (with 2 sts of next triangle).
Rows 8, 10, and 12 Repeat Row 2.
Row 14 Repeat Row 6. ** Do not turn. Pick up and purl 11 sts along side of next triangle. * Repeat from * to * 10 times more, then work from * to ** once. Turn work.

Tier 3
MAKE 12 RECTANGLES WITH D.

With RS facing, pick up and knit 12 sts along Rectangle 1 from Tier 2. * Slip last picked-up st to left-hand needle, ssk (picked-up st together with 1 st of next rectangle).

Row 1 and all WS rows Purl.
Rows 2, 4, and 6 Knit to last st, ssk.
Row 8 Knit to last st, SSSK.
Rows 10, 12, and 14 Repeat Row 2.
Row 16 Repeat Row 8. ** Do not turn. Pick up and knit 12 sts along side of next rectangle. * Repeat from * to * 10 times more, then work from * to ** once. Turn work.

CLASSIC ELITE Maya (50% llama, 50% wool; 1¾oz/50g; 82yds/74m) Green (A), Purple (B), Orange (C), Pink (D), Gold (E)

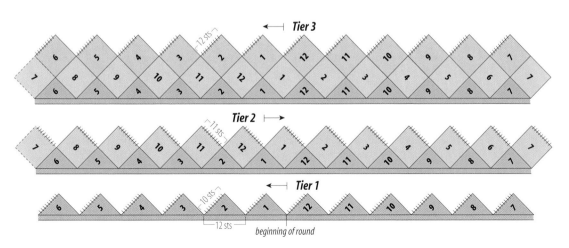

Tier 3

Tier 2

Tier 1

beginning of round

3

Tier 4

MAKE 12 RECTANGLES WITH E.

With WS facing, pick up and purl 12 sts along Rectangle 1 from previous tier.
* Slip last picked-up st to left-hand needle, p2tog.

Row 1 and all RS rows Knit.

Rows 2, 6, 8, 12, and 14 Purl to last st, p2tog.

Rows 4, 10, and 16 Purl to last st, p3tog.

** Do not turn. Pick up and purl 12 sts along side of next triangle. * Repeat from * to * 10 times more, then work from * to ** once. Turn work.

Tier 5

MAKE 12 RECTANGLES WITH B.

With RS facing, pick up and knit 12 sts along Rectangle 1 from Tier 4. * Slip last picked-up st to left-hand needle, ssk.

Row 1 and all WS rows Purl.

Rows 2, 6, 8, 12, and 14 Knit to last st, ssk.

Rows 4, 10, and 16 Knit to last st, SSSK.

** Do not turn. Pick up and knit 12 sts along side of next rectangle. * Repeat from * to * 10 times more, then work from * to ** once. Turn work.

Tier 6

MAKE 12 RECTANGLES WITH C.

With C, work as for Tier 4.

Note Work remaining odd-numbered tiers as for Tier 5, and remaining even-numbered tiers as for Tier 4, with the exceptions noted for each tier.

Tier 7

MAKE 12 RECTANGLES WITH A.

Pick up and knit 11 sts. Work 14 rows, ending Rows 2, 6, 10 and 14 with SSSK and all other even-numbered rows with ssk.

Tier 8

MAKE 12 RECTANGLES WITH D.

Pick up and purl 10 sts. Work 14 rows, ending Rows 4, 8 and 14 with p3tog and all other even-numbered rows with p2tog.

Tier 9

MAKE 12 RECTANGLES WITH E.

Pick up and knit 9 sts. Work 12 rows, ending Rows 4, 8, and 12 with SSSK and all other even-numbered rows with ssk.

Tier 10

MAKE 12 RECTANGLES WITH B.

Pick up and purl 8 sts. Work 12 rows, ending Rows 4 and 12 with p3tog and all other even-numbered rows with p2tog.

Tier 11

MAKE 12 RECTANGLES WITH C.

Pick up and knit 7 sts. Work 10 rows, ending Rows 4 and 10 with SSSK and all other even-numbered rows with ssk.

Tier 12

MAKE 12 RECTANGLES WITH A.

Pick up and purl 6 sts. Work 8 rows, ending Rows 4 and 8 with p3tog and all other even-numbered rows with p2tog.

Tier 13

MAKE 12 RECTANGLES WITH D.

Pick up and knit 5 sts. Work 6 rows, ending Rows 2 and 6 with SSSK and Row 4 with ssk.

BROWN SHEEP COMPANY
*Lamb's Pride Bulky (85% wool, 15%
mohair; 4oz/113g; 125yds/114m)*

MOUNTAIN COLORS 3 Ply
Montana Wool (100% Wool;
4oz/113g; 150yds/136m)

Tier 14
MAKE 12 RECTANGLES WITH E.

Pick up and purl 4 sts. Work 6 rows, ending Row 6 with p3tog and all other even-numbered rows with p2tog.

Tier 15
MAKE 12 RECTANGLES WITH B.

Pick up and knit 3 sts. Work 4 rows, ending Row 4 with SSSK and Row 2 with ssk—36 sts.

Cut yarn. Run yarn through sts, pull tightly and secure.

Straps (Make 2)
With dpns and A, cast on 2 sts.

Row 1 (WS) Knit.

Row 2 [Knit into front and back of st (Inc 1)] 2 times—4 sts.

Rows 3 and 5 Knit.

Row 4 Inc 1, knit to last st, Inc 1—6 sts.

Repeat Rows 4 and 5 once—8 sts. Knit 4 rows.

Work I-cord
*Next row K8, do not turn. Slide sts to opposite end of needle; repeat from * until strap measures 34". Turn work. Knit 4 rows, then work as follows:

Rows 1, 3, and 5 (WS) Knit.

Row 2 Ssk, k4, k2tog—6 sts.

Row 4 Ssk, k2, k2tog—4 sts.

Row 6 Ssk, k2tog—2 sts.

Row 7 Knit. Bind off.

Finishing
Felt pieces. Block by stretching over a suitably-sized cylindrical object (original sample was blocked over a large, metal, popcorn tin). Allow to dry completely. Steam if desired. Sew on straps.

When felted, the fabric no longer looks or acts like a knit. A felted bag does not stretch, stitches are no longer visible, and the colors blend; tote knit of handpainted yarn before felting, right, and after, left and below.

FELTING

To protect your washer from excess fiber, place bag in a zippered pillow protector or fine mesh bag. Set washer for hot wash, low water level and maximum agitation. (Using the rinse and spin cycles is not recommended as they may set permanent creases.) Add a small amount of mild detergent, and two old towels (non-shedding) or pairs of jeans for abrasion. Check on the progress about every 5 minutes. Every time you check the progress, pull the bag into shape and smooth the handle. Reset the washer to continue agitating if necessary. Do not let it drain and spin. When you are happy with the size, remove bag from the washer. Rinse thoroughly by hand in cool to warm water. Roll in towels to remove as much water as possible. (Or, for small bags, consider felting by hand. Just dip the knitting in hot, soapy water and then in cold water, rubbing vigorously between each dip. Repeat as many times as necessary until fabric felts.)

Pull bag into shape, flatten bottom and smooth handle. Allow to dry completely. Once dry, it may need some grooming to remove any extra fuzz or clumps of wool.

Try your hand at machine felting and then try some needle felting as well. The flap closes with a snap and the stripe is embellished with a contrasting swirl in needle felt.

Designed by Laura Kochevar

Flaps

it's easy ...go for it!

EASY

10" wide x 10" high x 3" deep, after felting

10cm/4"

21

16

• over stockinette stitch (knit on RS, purl on WS), before felting, using size 6mm/US10 needles

1 2 3 **4** 5 6

• Medium weight
MC • approximately 400 yds
CC • approximately 120 yds

• 5 and 6mm/US8 and 10, or size to obtain gauge

&

• Yarn needle, ½" magnetic snap, scrap of fabric and matching thread, ¼" cotton cording (braided 1 yd), felting needle, piece of upholstery foam 2" thick

Front

With larger needles and MC, cast on 75 sts. Work 24 rows in St st. Piece measures approximately 4½" from beginning. Decrease 1 st each side on next row, then every 8th row 10 times more, AT SAME TIME, work 12 more rows with MC (36 rows total), 22 rows with CC, then 50 rows with MC. Piece measures approximately 20½" from beginning. Bind off remaining 53 sts loosely.

Back

Work as for Front until piece measures 20½" from beginning—53 sts.

Work flap

Continuing with MC, decrease 1 st each side on next 3 rows—47 sts. Work 21 rows even. Flap measures approximately 4½". Decrease 1 st each side every row 19 times—9 sts. Bind off loosely.

Strap

With smaller needles and MC, cast on 6 sts. Work in St st until strap measures 35". Bind off. With yarn needle and MC, whipstitch sides of strap together, placing cotton cording between curled edges as you go. Scrunch the strap to fit length of cording. Close ends of strap.

Finishing

Lightly block edges of bag with steam iron to reduce curling. Sew side and bottom edges, matching stripes. Turn bag inside out. Sew straps to inside seams, beginning 1"-2" inside bag. With side seam facing you, flatten the bottom of the bag, forming a triangular gusset on each side approximately 3" deep. Sew across their bases, fold the triangles in toward each other and sew them down. Turn bag right side out. Sew snap, centered inside flap, approximately 1" from edge and matching location on front of bag. Felt bag and strap, as instructed on page 7.

Needle felting

Make sure bag is completely dry before needle felting (wet wool will cause the needles to break). Place a piece of upholstery foam inside purse. Place scraps of yarn on stripe in helix pattern. (You will need a longer piece of yarn than the pattern, as the yarn will "shrink" when felted.) Stab yarn at ¼" intervals to set the design, then stab along the yarn to set the pattern. Stray fibers can be coaxed into place with the tip of the needle. If desired, sew fabric to inside for pocket.

Helix Pattern

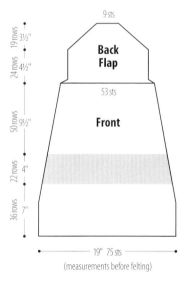

Back Flap

9 sts

3½" 19 rows

4½" 24 rows

53 sts

Front

9½" 50 rows

4" 22 rows

7" 36 rows

19" 75 sts

(measurements before felting)

PATONS Classic Merino (100% wool;
3½oz/100g; 223yds/204m)

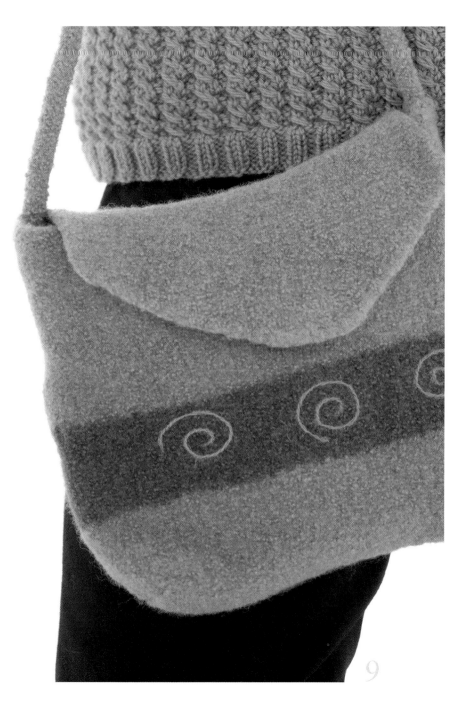

9

Durable and practical, felting is perfect for handbags. This bag features a snap closure and a simple stripe pattern. It will make a wonderful gift for someone you love.

Designed by Laura Kochevar

Snaps

EASY

15" wide x 12" high x 4" deep,
after felting

10cm/4"

21

16

• over stockinette stitch
(knit on RS, purl on WS), before felting
using larger needles

1 2 3 **4** 5 6

• Medium weight
MC • 405 yds
CC • 405 yds

• 5 and 6mm/US8 and 10,
or size to obtain gauge

&

• Yarn needle, ½" magnetic snap, scrap of
ultrasuede fabric and matching thread,
4 large grommets, ¼" cotton cording
(braided, not plied, 2 yds)

Front

With larger needles and MC, cast on 90 sts. Work 24 rows in St st. Piece measures approximately 4½" from beginning. Decrease 1 st each side on next row, then every 10th row 10 times more, AT SAME TIME, continue working color pattern as follows: Work 24 more rows with MC (48 rows total), then work 1 row CC, 13 rows MC, 2 rows CC, 8 rows MC, 3 rows CC, 5 rows MC, 5 rows CC, 3 rows MC, 8 rows CC, 2 rows MC, 13 rows CC, 1 row MC, 17 rows CC. Piece measures approximately 24½" from beginning. Bind off remaining 68 sts loosely.

Back

Work as for Front.

Strap

Work as for Strap on p. 8 EXCEPT work until Strap measures 82".

Finishing

Follow Finishing and Needle Felting instructions on p. 8 EXCEPT don't attach Strap until after felting.

Grommets

Place top edge of grommets approximately 1" below top edge of felted tote and insert according to packet directions. Place 2 grommets on each side. Thread strap through grommet holes and stitch ends together firmly. Sew snap, centered inside bag, approximately 1½" from top edge.

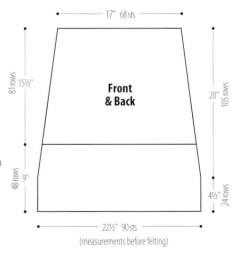

17" 68 sts

81 rows 15½"

Front
& Back

20"

105 rows

48 rows 9"

4½"

24 rows

22½" 90 sts

(measurements before felting)

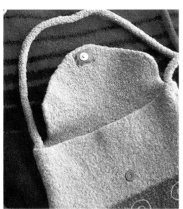

Magnetic snaps attach with prongs on the back of each piece. The prongs go through slits in the fabric and into a backing plate, then they are bent to secure the snap. The prongs and plate are meant to be hidden between layers of fabric, but since most felted bags have no lining, first attach the snaps to small squares of fabric or suede, then sew the squares onto the bags.

PATONS Classic Merino (100% wool; 3½oz/100g; 223yds/204m) Black (MC), Red (CC)

Less than 200 yards of yarn, a trip to the washing machine, and a little needling, result in a fun felted pocketbook.

Designed by Bev Galeskas

Felted Pocketbook

INTERMEDIATE

7" wide x 5" high, after felting

10cm/4"

18

14

• over stockinette stitch
(knit every round), before felting

1 2 3 4 **5** 6

• Bulky weight
• 170 yds

• 6.5mm/US10½, or size to obtain gauge,
40cm (16") long

• Two 8mm/US11 double-pointed
needles (dpn)

• Stitch marker, 38-gauge and 40-gauge
felting needles, small amounts of
contrasting-color fleece, small piece of
thick foam

12

Note

See *Techniques*, p. 80, for ssk, Make 1 (M1), and I-cord.

PURSE

With circular needle, cast on 42 sts. Place marker, join and work in rounds as follows:

Shape bottom of bag

Rounds 1, 3, 5, 7 Purl.

Round 2 K1, * M1, k1, M1, k18, M1, k1, M1 *, k1, repeat from * to * once—50 sts.

Round 4 K2, * M1, k1, M1, k20, M1, k1 M1 *, k3, repeat from * to * once, k1—58 sts.

Round 6 K3, * M1, k1, M1, k22, M1, k1, M1 *, k5, repeat from * to * once, k2—66 sts. Work 42 rounds in St st. [Purl 1 round, knit 1 round] twice. Purl 1 round. Before working bind-off row, mark beginning of round with a pin, below the needle. Count over 33 sts and mark for other side edge. These markers are used for strap placement. Bind off.

Bottom edging

Turn bag upside down and slip circular needle into the purl loops from Round 7 of bottom of bag—66 loops on needle. Join yarn and knit 1 round. Bind off knitwise.

Closure tab

With circular needle, cast on 8 sts. Work back and forth in rows as follows:

Row 1 K6, sl 2 sts purlwise with yarn in front (wyif).

Row 2 Taking yarn firmly across the back of the 2 sl sts, k6, sl 2 wyif.
Repeat Row 2 until piece measures 4½" from beginning.

Buttonhole row K2, k2tog, yo 2 times, ssk, sl 2.

Next row K3, knit into front and back of double yo, k1, sl 2.

Next 2 rows K6, sl 2.

Decrease row K2, [k2tog] 2 times, sl 2—6 sts.

Next row K4, sl 2.

Decrease row K1, [k2tog] 2 times, sl 1—4 sts.

Decrease row [K2tog] 2 times, pass first st over 2nd st.
Fasten off remaining sts.

Strap

With dpns and 2 strands yarn held together, cast on 4 sts. Work I-cord for 15". Bind off.

Finishing

Sew cast-on edges together to close bottom of bag. Sew one end of strap to inside of bag at side marker, extending the end down into bag approximately 1½". Sew other end at 2nd marker. Pin closure tab centered on back of bag, with the bottom of the tab approximately 1½" from top edge of bag. Sew tab to bag, sewing around 3 sides of tab, then sewing across tab (parallel to top edge of bag) to secure. Felt bag (see p. 7). Needle felt design using fiber for circles and yarn for detail.

Felted button

Make a soft ball of fleece approximately 1" in diameter (or twice the diameter of the finished button). With damp fingers, smooth the surface. Add a few drops of detergent to a small bowl of warm water. Dip the ball into this and roll briskly between the palms of your hands. Check the surface from time to time, smoothing as needed and continue rolling until you have a firm, round felted ball. Rinse under running water and allow to dry. Use a large, sharp darning needle to pierce a hole through the bottom quarter of the button for sewing. Sew button to bag using a small, sharp needle and heavy-duty thread.

BROWN SHEEP COMPANY
Lamb's Pride Worsted (85% wool,
15% mohair; 4oz/115g; 190yds/173m)

Needle Felting

Bev Galeskas

Detail

Felting needles come to us from the commercial fabric industry where thousands are used together in mechanized beds to make everything from felt fabric to quilt batting. In recent years, fiber artists have been using them to create dolls, bears, and other three-dimensional art. Felting needles can also be used to embellish your felted knits. These fine, barbed needles allow you to literally paint with fibers.

Needle felting is a completely dry technique. Rather than shocking the fibers with water and agitation, the little barbs positioned near the needle point do the work. You can feel them by gently running your fingernail along the shaft of the needle. When the needle is stabbed through fiber, small amounts are caught on these barbs and carried into the fiber or fabric below. Since all the barbs are pointed downwards, the fiber is left behind when the needle is removed. A few stabs will create a temporary bond and stabbing repeatedly, or "needling" will permanently bond the fibers together.

Felting needles come in a variety of sizes (gauges) and point shapes. The smaller the gauge number, the larger (in diameter) the needle. A good all-purpose size is a 38-gauge. Triangular points are the most common, but you might also want to try the slightly more expensive star points. With four barbed sides instead of three, these will bond fibers at a slightly faster rate. A larger, 36-gauge needle is good for preliminary work on a large design, but it will leave visible puncture holes, so switch to a fine 40-gauge needle to get a smooth finish.

Wool fleece, in either top or roving form, is most commonly used for needle felting. Packages with small amounts of mixed colors are available for this purpose. Yarn can also be used, both as is for outlines or lettering, or pulled apart into bits of fluff and used like fleece. A worsted or bulky singles wool yarn is especially easy to untwist and pull apart.

There is no need to limit yourself to fibers that would felt by conventional wet-felting methods. Take a look at your stash or scrap bag and try needle felting with other fibers, even novelty yarns.

Besides needles and fiber, it is important to use a piece of foam to protect your worktable and avoid breaking needle points or worse yet, stabbing your knee. Starter kits come with a square of thick foam. An old foam pillow or thick sponge may be substituted. To work on a small purse like the one shown here, you will need a piece of foam or sponge to fit inside the purse, to keep the two sides separated.

1 Plan your design.
2 Place your foam under the felt.

3 Lay out fibers for the larger areas (don't worry yet about fine details or exact shaping, that will come later).

4 Using your felting needle, stab the fiber a couple of times to tack it in place on the felt. Stab straight in and just deep enough for the barbs to pass into the felt fabric. Stabbing too deeply will only carry fiber into the foam.

5 Use a pair of tweezers or a double-pointed needle to arrange fibers as you work. Do not try to move the fibers with the felting needle as this may break the point. Continue to tack fibers into place, stabbing only enough times to secure them. If you don't like the position of the fiber, simply pull it off and reposition it.
6 Once the area of your design is placed, it is time to fine-tune the shape and "needle" it permanently into place. Use tweezers or a double-pointed needle to push or pull fibers into place and to smooth the edges. Remember to stab straight down and not too deeply, working over the entire surface until it is firmly attached.
7 Add fiber to blend colors or fill thin spots as needed. If you find too much fiber in one place, use tweezers to pull some off, then needle the surface again to smooth it.

8 Add colors, outlines, and any other finishing details as your design progresses. Switch to a finer, 40-gauge needle for the final finishing step and a smoother surface.
9 For an even smoother finish, you may want to wet-felt the surface of your design. Mix a small amount of Woolmix or other rinse-free wool wash in some water and use your hand to rub it into the surface. There is no need to soak the work, just buff the surface with the solution. When you have the finish you desire, blot with towels and allow to dry.

One pattern/three gauges. *The idea is simple: knit a square bottom for the bag; pick up stitches around this square and knit in the round, adding increases to form the front, back, and side panels; finally, knit two top sections and add handles.*

Designed by Ginger Luters

Three for the Road

INTERMEDIATE

Small bag • 8" wide x 6" high
Medium bag • 10½" wide x 9½" high
Large bag • 19" wide x 15" high

10cm/4"
37, 25, 16 GET CLOSE
21, 18, 10
• over stockinette st (knit all rounds)

1 2 3·4·5 6

• Light weight • 140 yds
• Medium weight • 165 yds
• Bulky weight • 300 yds

• 4mm/US6 • 5mm/US8 • 8mm/US11,
or size to obtain gauge, 60cm (24") long

• 3.5mm (E) • 3.75mm (F) • 4mm (G)

&

• Zipper, stitch markers
• One button, approx 1¼–1½"

Notes

1 See *Techniques,* p. 80, for ssk, picking up stitches, crochet chain, I-cord, and grafting. *2* Slip sts purlwise with yarn in back. *3* Finish with knitted straps or attach purchased handles; instructions for both are provided.

BAG
Base
Cast on 23 sts. Knit 44 rows, slipping the first st of every row.
Sides
Next row (RS) K23 (for Front Panel), place marker (pm), then pick up and knit 22 sts along side edge (for Side Panel), pm, 23 sts along cast-on edge (for Back Panel), pm, 22 sts along side edge (for Side Panel), place contrasting marker for beginning of round (see illustration)—90 sts. Join and work in rounds as follows:
Rounds 1–2 Knit.
Round 3 K23, * sl 1, knit next st then knit into left loop of st below (LL1, see illustration), knit to 2 sts before marker, knit into right loop of st in row below next st then knit st on

needle (RL1, see illustration), sl 1; repeat from *—4 sts increased.
Round 4 Knit.
Round 5 * Knit to marker, sl 1, knit to 1 st before marker, sl 1; repeat from *.
Round 6 Repeat Round 4.
Repeat Rounds 3–6, 9 times more—130 sts. Place first 88 sts on hold, leaving 42 sts on needle.

Top sections (worked back and forth)
Row 1 (WS) Slip first st from holder to left-hand (LH) needle and k2tog with next st on needle, knit to last st, sl 1, slip last st from holder to right-hand (RH) needle, sl 2 unworked sts on RH needle back to LH needle and ssk.
Row 2 Knit.
Repeat Rows 1 and 2, 10 times more—110 sts (including sts on holder).
Next row (WS) Bind off as follows: K2tog (first st on needle with first st on holder), bind off until 1 st remains on LH needle, ssk last st on needle with last st on holder, bind off remaining sts—66 sts on a second holder. Place 24 sts on a separate holder, 42 sts on needle ready to work a WS row, leaving remaining 24 sts on first holder. Work Rows 1 and 2, using sts from appropriate holder, 12 times—22 sts

knit across these 23 sts

pick up 22 sts along side edge

Base

pick up 22 sts along side edge

x = markers

pick up 23 sts along cast on edge

Right lifted increase

Knit into right loop of stitch in row below next stitch on left needle (1), then knit stitch on needle (2).

RLI

Left lifted increase

Knit one stitch, then knit into left loop of stitch in row below last stitch knitted (3).

LLI

Large bag: DYED IN THE WOOL Hand Painted Mop Cord 00% cotton; 375g/13oz; 205m/225yds)

17

The front and back panels are each 23 stitches wide by 42 rows tall. Try one of these or plan your own knit/purl pattern for these panels.

23 sts

☐ Knit
▨ Purl

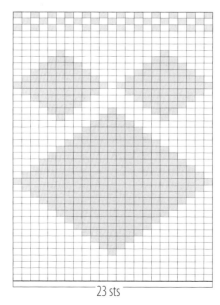

23 sts

attach crochet chain

top sections ── pick up handle sts

side section ── sew button

back panel   front panel

(including 1 st on each holder).

Next row (WS) Bind off as for other Top.

Straps

Pick up and knit 5 sts in upper right corner of Front Panel (see diagram). Work for 28" in St st.

Decrease row (RS) Knit to last 2 sts, k2tog. Repeat Decrease row every RS row until 1 st remains. Fasten off. Work 3 more straps in remaining corners.

Handles

Pick up stitches as follows, depending on the style of handle you purchase: across top of Front and Back Panels (for tan bag), or for a tab at each end of top of Front and Back Panels (for blue bag). Work back and forth in stockinette stitch (k on RS, p on WS) for 1 to 2" for a casing. Fold WS together, insert handle, and graft casing stitches to bag.

Finishing

Sew zipper into top opening. Work a 4½" crochet chain button loop at center top of Back Panel (see illustration). Sew button on center top of Front Panel. If using straps, tie front straps together using a square knot, at desired length; repeat for back straps. Weave in all loose ends.

Small tan bag
BERROCO Suede (100% nylon
1¾oz/50g; 120yds/111m)
Medium blue bag
ROWAN Pronto (50% cotton, 50% acrylic
1¾oz/50g; 55yds/50m)

Zippers

Sewing a zipper into a knit can seem daunting to the uninitiated. Although the knitted fabric has stretch, the zipper does not, and the two must be joined as neatly as possible to prevent ripples. Follow these steps for a smooth installation.

1 Measure the length of the opening. Select a zipper the length of the opening in the color of your choice. If you can't find that exact length, choose one that is a bit longer.

2 Pre-shrink your zipper in the method you will use to clean the garment. Wash and dry it or carefully steam it (you don't want to melt the teeth if they are plastic or nylon).

3 Place the zipper in opening, aligning each side. Allow extra length to extend at lower end.

4 Pin in place. Be generous with the pins, and take all the time you need. Extra care taken here makes the next steps easier.

5 Baste in place. When you are satisfied with the placement, remove the pins.

6 Sew in the zipper, making neat, even stitches that are firm enough to withstand use.

7 Sew a stop at end of zipper and clip excess off if necessary.

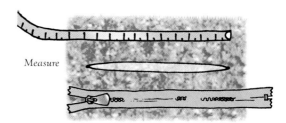

Measure

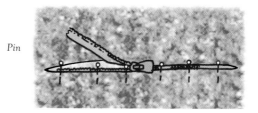

Pin

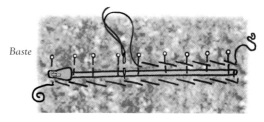

Baste

Sew in

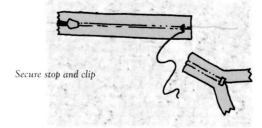

Secure stop and clip

Add a little refinement: A button and loop
attached to the edge of the top sections keep things tidy.

Make a simple bag from a tube. But rather than placing the zipper parallel to the bottom seam, rotate it 90° within the opening. The result is a bag with added dimension and character. Add a strap, a loop, and maybe the optional button for a bag with different personalities.

Designed by Knitter's Design Team

SoHo Sling

it's
easy
...go
for it!

EASY

16" circumference x 8" high
• approximately

10cm/4"

28–32 ▥ GET CLOSE
22–24
• over stockinette stitch
(knit every round)

1 2 **3-4** 5 6

• Light–Medium weight
•180 yds

• 3.5–4mm/US4–6, or size to obtain
gauge, 40cm/16" long

&

• One extra needle for 3-needle bind-off
• Zipper, needle, thread
• Beaded fringe, optional

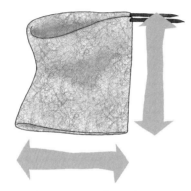

1 Cast on 90 stitches and join.
Knit a tube half as tall as the circumference.

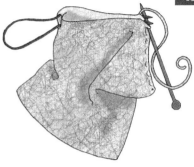

2 Divide stitches onto two needles, turn work WS out, and work 3-needle bind-off (see p. 83).

3 Turn to RS, lay flat, and place markers at center front (CF) and back of opening (CB).

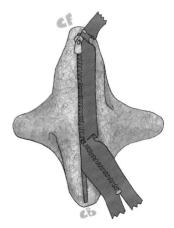

4 Set in zipper so tab will be center front when closed.

Need help with the zipper? Turn to p. 21.

BERROCO INC *Denim Silk* (80% rayon, 20% silk; 1¾oz/50g; 105yds/97m)

SoHo Sling

7 Add loop at center front, add optional button at lower corner.

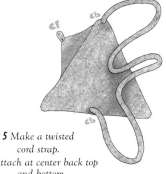

5 Make a twisted cord strap.
6 Attach at center back top and bottom.

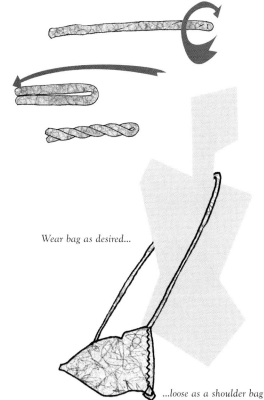

Wear bag as desired...

...loose as a shoulder bag

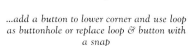

...add a button to lower corner and use loop as buttonhole or replace loop & button with a snap

...pull strap thru loop for another look.

...or add beaded fringe. Purchase it at the fabric store and work it into the bag. Do so in the final round, prior to bind-off. Knit a stitch or two, pull a fringe through from WS to RS, repeat around, then proceed as above.

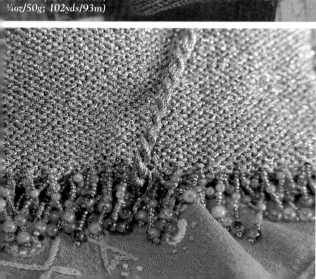

N Denim (100% cotton;
¾oz/50g; 102yds/93m)

ROWAN Lurex Shimmer
(80% viscose/20% polyester; .9oz/25g; 104yds/95m)

Try patchwork knitting on a small scale. Knit this classic pocketbook style in the suggested colors, or choose your own combination from a palette that suits your wardrobe.

Designed by Shanta Moitra

Pocketbook in Blocks

INTERMEDIATE
11½" wide x 8" high x 2" deep

10cm/4"

32

23

• over stockinette stitch (knit on RS, purl on WS) using larger needles

1 2 3 **4** 5 6

• Medium weight
A • 170 yds
B • 340 yds
C • 85 yds

• 3.5 and 4.5mm/US4 and 7, or size to obtain gauge

• Two 3.5mm /US4 double-pointed needles (dpn)

&

• Cable needle (cn), stitch holders, snap, ½ yd lining fabric

Basic mitered square

With A, cast on or pick up (depending on where you are) 22 sts.
Row 1 (WS) K10, k2tog, k10.
Row 2 With B, k9, S2KP2, k9.
Rows 3, 5 Purl.
Row 4 K8, S2KP2, k8.
Row 6 With A, k7, S2KP2, k7.
Row 7 Knit.
Row 8 With C, k6, S2KP2, k6.
Rows 9, 11 Purl.
Row 10 K5, S2KP2, k5.
Row 12 With A, k4, S2KP2, k4.
Row 13 Knit.
Row 14 With B, k3, S2KP2, k3.
Rows 15, 17 Purl.
Row 16 K2, S2KP2, k2.
Row 18 With A, k1, S2KP2, k1.
Row 19 Knit.
Row 20 S2KP2. Fasten off last st.
Basic mitered square measures approximately 2".

2-square module

With A, cast on or pick up (depending on where you are) 22 sts place marker (pm), cast on or pick up 22 sts—44 sts. Work as for Basic Mitered Square, working each row of instructions twice. Bind off remaining 2 sts.

Notes

1 See *Techniques*, p. 80 for ssk, S2KP2, cable cast-on, picking up stitches, I-cord, grafting stitches, and 3-needle bind-off.
2 Use cable cast-on throughout. ***3*** Pick up sts with RS of work facing, smaller needles, and A.

PURSE

Tier 1 (3-module tier)
Module 1 With smaller needles and A, cast on 44 sts. Work 2-Square Module.
Module 2 Pick up and knit 11 sts along left edge of module just completed then cast on 33 sts—44 sts. Work 2-Square Module.
Module 3 Work as for Module 2.
Tier 2 (4-module tier)
Module 4 Pick up and knit 11 sts along top edge of Module 1, ending at center of module, then cast on 11 sts—22 sts. Work Basic Mitered Square.
Modules 5 and 6 * Pick up and knit 11 sts along left edge of square just completed and 22 sts from center top of module to center of next module, then cast on 11 sts—44 sts. Work 2-Square Module. Repeat from * for Module 6.

BERROCO *Smart Cotton (68% cotton, 29% rayon, 3% nylon; 1¾oz/50g; 87yds/80m) Beige (A), Navy (B), Green (C)*

Basic Mitered Square

11 sts

11 sts

2- Square Module

11 sts ⎯ 11 sts

22 sts

2	7	6	5	4
1	3	2	1	

⎯⎯ *Cast on*

- - - *Pick up and knit*

Module 7 Pick up and knit 11 sts along left edge of Module 6 and 11 sts along top of Module 3—22 sts. Work Basic Mitered Square.

Continue to alternate a 3-module tier and a 4-module tier until a total of 12 tiers have been worked.

Side gusset (make 2)

With larger needles and B, cast on 17 sts. Work Side Gusset Chart until piece measures 8". Place sts on hold.

Finishing

Block pieces. Line bag as follows: Cut a piece of lining fabric 25" long × 13" wide. With iron, press ½" seam allowances on all sides. Sew lining to inside of purse.

I-cord edging and gusset joining

With dpn and B, cast on 3 sts, then beginning at center front of purse (point A on diagram), * pick up and knit 1 st along edge—4 sts on needle, do not turn, slide sts to opposite end of needle, k2, ssk; repeat from * to corner (point B), ending with 3 sts on needle. Join side gusset to purse between points B and C as follows: with WS together and sts on hold at top of purse, continue working I-cord as before, but pick up sts along edge through both purse and gusset. In same way, join bottom of gusset to purse between points C and D. Join other side of gusset to purse between points D and E. Work I-cord edging as before along edges of flap (between points E and F). Join other side gusset to purse between points F and G,

G and H, and H and I. Work edging along remaining half of front edge, ending at point A. Graft ends of cord together.

Shoulder strap

With RS facing, larger needles and B, continue Side Gusset Pattern over 17 gusset sts on hold until strap measures 17", place sts on hold. Repeat for other side. Join strap sts, using 3-needle bind-off. Fold outer edges of strap to inside and sew edges together at center (leaving enough ease at gusset so that gusset doesn't fold). Sew snap on front and inside of flap.

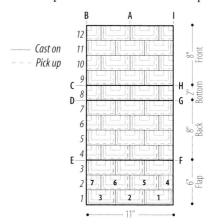

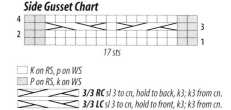

Side Gusset Chart

17 sts

☐ K on RS, p on WS
▨ P on RS, k on WS
3/3 RC sl 3 to cn, hold to back, k3; k3 from cn.
3/3 LC sl 3 to cn, hold to front, k3; k3 from cn.

ADDITIONAL COLORWAYS

This patchwork pocketbook can take on many looks, depending on the colorway you choose. For a soft, summery effect, try one in lavender and greens. Bold graphics can be achieved with a more highly contrasting combo. Or sample your own colorway by wrapping a card with the colors you love. Remember, a dark-colored separator gives a more intense look than a pale one.

Place a mitered square on one point and fold back another for a bag with stripes that go in all directions. The knitting is easy and the felting is fun.

Designed by Joan McGowan-Michael

On Pointe Handbag

INTERMEDIATE

12" wide (at widest point) x 8" high x
3½" deep , after felting

10cm/4"

32

16
• over garter stitch (knit every row),
before felting

1 2 **3** 4 5 6

• Light weight
A • 214 yds
B, C, D, E • 107 yds each

• 5.5mm/US9, or size to obtain gauge

• One 1¼"/32mm

• Yarn needle

99-Row Stripe Pattern

Rows	Color	Rows	Color
4 rows	C	6 rows	E
2 rows	B	4 rows	B
2 rows	A	2 rows	D
6 rows	D	4 rows	A
4 rows	E	2 rows	C
2 rows	C	2 rows	B
4 rows	A	4 rows	D
6 rows	B	6 rows	E
4 rows	D	4 rows	C
4 rows	C	27 rows	D

Note

See *Techniques*, p. 80, for invisible cast-on and grafting.

Square (make 2)

With C, cast on 101 sts. Work 99-row Stripe Pattern, AT SAME TIME, work shaping as follows:

Row 1 (RS) K49, k3tog, k49.

Row 2 and all WS rows Knit.

Row 3 K48, k3tog, k48.

Continue working 1 fewer knit st at each side of center k3tog on every RS row until 3 sts remain, ending with pattern row 98.

Row 99 K3tog. Fasten off last st.

Gusset
Note

Do not work Stripe Pattern; change color as desired, leaving enough of color A to work strap.

Cast on 20 sts. Work in garter stitch until piece measures 35". Bind off. Sew gusset onto lower portion of squares (illustration 1), beginning and ending at 40th row of Stripe Pattern on each side.

Strap

With A, invisibly cast on 10 sts. Work in St st (knit on RS, purl on WS) for 325 rows. Graft open sts to cast-on sts to create a circle.

Finishing

Create a tuck in center of gusset (illustration 2) and place strap inside tuck, then sew sides of tuck together over strap (leaving strap free to move). Work in same way on other side. Felt (see p. 7). With yarn needle and A, work blanket stitch (illustration 3) along edges of flaps. Sew decorative button to each flap.

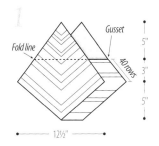

1

Fold line

Gusset

40 rows

5"

3"

5"

12½"

Sew gusset to squares.

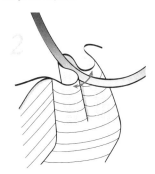

2

Place strap into tuck at side of bag and sew sides of tuck together over strap.

3

Work blanket stitch along edges of flap.

JO SHARP 100% Pure Wool (100% wool; 1¾oz/50g; 107yds/98m) Camel (A), Orange (B), Ivory (C), Red (D), and Gold (E)

Spice-colored stripes edged in black give this striking fabric an ethnic feel. Straightforward construction puts the focus on color, so finishing the practical bag is a snap.

Designed by Megan Lacey

Market Stripes

INTERMEDIATE
20" circumference x 9" high

10cm/4"

27

21

• over stockinette stitch
(knit on RS, purl on WS)

1 2 3 **4** 5 6

• Medium weight
MC • 105 yds
A, B, C, D, E, F, G • 30 yds each
H • 80 yds

• 4.5mm/US7 double-pointed needles (dpn),
or size to obtain gauge

• 4.5mm/US7, 40cm (16") long

&

• Stitch marker, yarn needle

BAG
Note
See *Techniques*, p. 80, for ssk, invisible cast-on, grafting, and I-cord.

Purse
With A, cast on 40 sts using invisible cast-on. Work Rows 5–64 of Chart Pattern, then work Rows 1–64, and work Rows 1–3 once more. With A, graft open sts on needle to cast-on row to form a tube.

Top band
With RS facing, circular needle, and MC, pick up and knit 110 sts evenly along left side edge of purse. Place marker, join, and work in rounds as follows:
Rounds 1–4 * P1, k1; repeat from *.
Round 5 (eyelet round) * [P1, k1] 4 times, yo, k2tog; repeat from *.
Rounds 6–9 Repeat Rounds 1–4. Bind off in rib.

Bottom piece
Note Change to dpn when necessary.
With RS facing, circular needle, and MC, pick up and knit 108 sts evenly around remaining edge of purse. Place marker, join, and work in rounds as follows:
Rounds 1–8 Purl.

Round 9 Fold band to inside and * with left-hand needle, pick up a st from pick-up row and purl this st together with next st on left-hand needle; repeat from *.
Round 10 Knit.
Begin decrease rounds:
Round 1 * K10, ssk; repeat from *.
Round 2 and all even-numbered rounds Knit.
Round 3 * K9, ssk; repeat from *.
Round 5 * K8, ssk; repeat from *.
Continue working decreases every other round (working one fewer st before decrease each time) until 9 sts remain. Cut yarn, run tail through remaining sts, pull tightly and secure on WS.

Drawstring
Use any color to make 4-st unattached I-cord 65" long. Bind off. Weave I-cord through eyelets in top band, ending at starting eyelet. Tie ends together in bow or knot.

DALE OF NORWAY *Free Style*
(100% wool; 1¾oz/50g; 88yds/80m)

Color key

- Black (MC)
- Orange (A)
- Navy (B)
- Red (C)
- Wine (D)
- Gold (E)
- Cherry (F)
- Lime (G)
- Sapphire (H)

Chart

2-st rep

Market Stripes

INTERMEDIATE

B **A**

STANDARD FIT

S (M, L, 1X, 2X)
A 36 (38, 42, 46, 48)"
B 18 (19¼, 20½, 22¾, 24)"

• For gauge see p. 32

1 2 3 **4** 5 6

• Medium weight
MC • 230 (255, 295, 350, 380) yds
A, B, C, D, E, F, G • 70 (75, 85, 95, 105) yds each
H • 55 (60, 65, 70, 75) yds

• 4.5mm/US7, or size to obtain gauge,
40cm and 60cm (16" and 24") long

• 4.5mm/US7 double-pointed
needles (dpn)

• Stitch markers and holders

VEST

Notes

1 See *Techniques*, p. 80, for 3-needle bind-off and attached I-cord. *2* For ease in working, circle numbers for your size.

Back

With A, cast on 94 (100, 110, 120, 126) sts. Work in Chart Pattern (p. 33) until piece measures approximately 8¼ (9½, 10¾, 13, 14¼)" from beginning, end with Chart Row 56 (64, 8, 24, 32).

Shape armholes

Next row (RS) Bind off 11 (11, 11, 11, 13) sts at beginning of next 2 rows—72 (78, 88, 98, 100) sts. Work 62 more rows of Chart Pattern, ending with Chart Row 56 (64, 8, 24, 32). Armhole measures approximately 9½". Place sts on hold.

Front

Work as for Back until 46 rows have been worked from beginning of Armhole shaping, ending with Chart Row 38 (46, 54, 6, 14). Armhole measures approximately 6¾".

Shape neck

Next row (RS) Work 25 (27, 31, 34, 34) sts, join 2nd ball of yarn and bind off center 22 (24, 26, 30, 32) sts, work to end. Working both sides at same time, decrease 1 st at each Neck edge every RS row 5 times—20 (22, 26, 29, 29) sts. Work 7 rows even, ending same as for Back. Place sts on hold.

Finishing

Block pieces. Join shoulders, using 3-needle bind-off.

Neckband

With RS facing, circular needle, MC and beginning at left shoulder, pick up and knit 14 sts evenly along left Front neck, 22 (24, 26, 30, 32) sts along center Front neck, 14 sts along right Front neck, and 32 (34, 36, 40, 42) sts along Back neck—82 (86, 90, 98, 102) sts. Place marker, join, and purl 1 round. Bind off knitwise. Sew side seams.

Lower edge and armhole bands

With RS facing, dpn, and MC, cast on 4 sts and work attached I-cord around lower and armhole edges.

Front
& Back

3¾ (4¼, 5, 5½, 5½)"

6 (6½, 7, 7½, 8)"

2¾"

9½"

15 (16¼, 17½, 19¾, 21)"

8¼ (9½, 10¾, 13, 14¼)"

18 (19, 21, 23, 24)"

Looking for just the bag to carry when you want to be noticed? Whether you choose jewel-toned, mercerized cottons or felted wool, the knitting is fun and the finishing is foolproof.

Designed by Lori Ihnen

Zigzag on the Town

INTERMEDIATE

Small bag: 19" circumference x 10" high
Large bag: 24" x 14" high

10cm/4"

31, 26

23, 16
• over stockinette st
(knit on RS, purl on WS)

1 2 **3-4** 5 6

• Light weight A • 200 yds
B, C, D, E • 100 yds each
• Medium weight • 400 yds

• 3.5mm/US4
• 5.5mm/US9
or size to obtain gauge, 40cm (16") long

&

• Stitch marker
• One extra needle:
3.5mm/US4
5.5mm/US9

Notes
1 See *Techniques*, p. 80, for ssk, SK2P, cable cast-on, 3-needle bind-off, and yo before a knit or purl st. **2** Bag is knit circularly from the top down. **3** For a multicolor yarn, follow zigzag chart without color changes.

BAG
With A, cable cast on 148 sts, place marker and join.
Begin Zigzag chart: Row 1 * K1, ssk, [k9, SK2P] 5 times, k9, k2tog; repeat from * once more. Continue as established for 77 rows of Zigzag chart, changing colors as indicated along left edge of chart.
Finishing
Turn bag inside out. Place 74 Front and Back sts on separate needles. Hold work so that yarn comes from front needle.
Next row With extra size 4 needle, knit first st from back needle, work 3-needle bind-off to last st on front needle, k1, pass first st over. Fasten off.
Shoulder strap
Cut 13 strands of yarn 5 yds long in the following colors: 8A, 2C, 1 each B, D, and E. Make a twisted cord (see p. 40). Sew cord to inside along each side from lower edge to just below Eyelet Round. If desired, machine stitch knotted end back and forth and cut off knot to reduce bulk.
Cut 3 strands of yarn 5 yds long in the following colors: 2A and 1C.
Drawstring
Make a twisted cord (see p. 40). Cut cord in half and knot ends. With RS of bag facing, begin at side of bag and lace one cord through yo's of Eyelet Round as follows: * Go in first eyelet and out next eyelet; repeat from * twice more, go in next eyelet, skip one eyelet and ** go out next eyelet, go in next eyelet; repeat from ** twice more, go out original eyelet. Repeat for other cord, beginning on opposite side of bag. To close bag, pull all ends and tie in front. Make twisted cord the desired length.

Zigzag chart

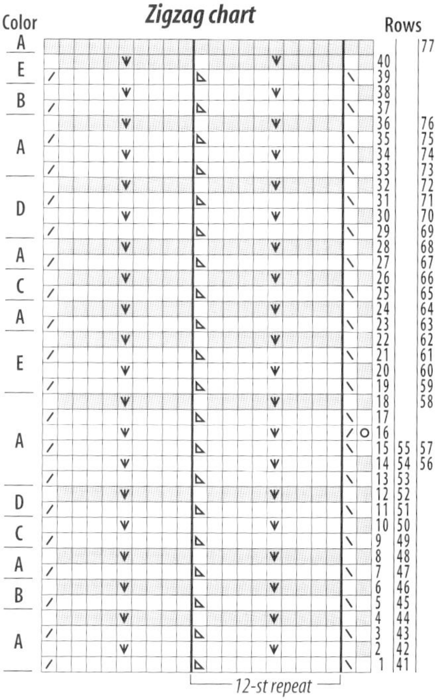
Color
Rows
12-st repeat

- Knit
- Purl
- K2tog
- Ssk
- K1, yo, k1 into st
- P1, yo, p1 into st
- SK2P
- Yo

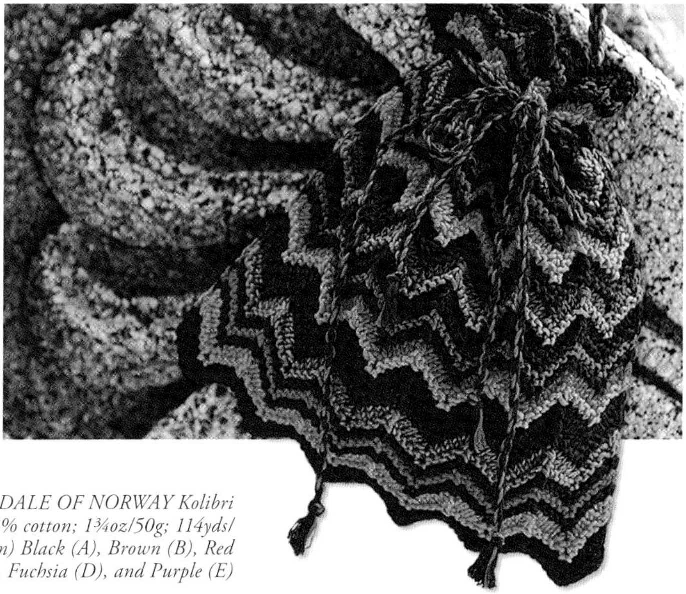

DALE OF NORWAY Kolibri (100% cotton; 1¾oz/50g; 114yds/105m) Black (A), Brown (B), Red (C), Fuchsia (D), and Purple (E)

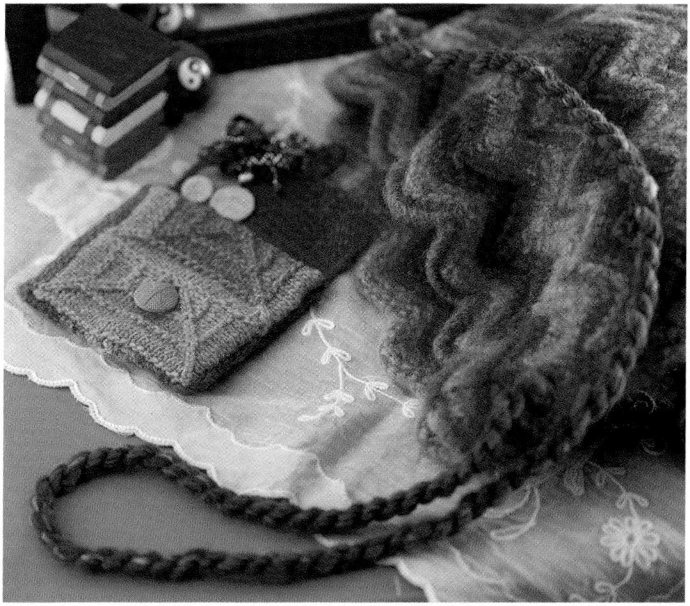

NORO Kureyon (100% wool, 1¾oz/50g; 110yds/100m)

For large felted bag, 200 yds of medium-weight wool, was worked with a needle 2 sizes larger than usual and felted to 24" circumference × 14" high

A strip of five 2-square modules (p. 26) makes the small felted clutch

Beautiful yarns often need simple applications. We accomplish that here with the Gallery Bags: take a palette of mixed colors with black accent or make a black bag with colorful accents. Finished with beaded closures, these bags are works of art.

Designed by Chris de Longpre

Gallery Bags

INTERMEDIATE

Small Bag 7½" wide x 7" high
Large Bag 13" wide x 10" high

10cm/4"

26
16
• over Pattern Stitch
using size 5mm/US8 needles

1 2 3 **4** 5 6

• Medium weight
A • 36 yds small bag (175 yds large bag)

1 2 **3** 4 5 6

• Light weight
B • 80 yds small bag (160 yds large bag)

• 5mm/US8, or size to obtain gauge

&
• beads for fringe
• optional lining materials

Pattern Stitch (over a multiple of 12 sts, plus 5)

Row 1 (WS) With MC, k5, * p7, k5; repeat from *.
Row 2 With CC, k5, * sl 7 sts purlwise with yarn in front (wyif), k5; repeat from *.
Row 3 With CC, repeat Row 1.
Row 4 With MC, knit.
Row 5 With MC, repeat Row 1.
Row 6 With MC, k8, * k1 under strand (see illustration), k11; repeat from *, end k1 under strand, k8.
Repeat Rows 1–6 for Pattern Stitch.

Notes

1 See *Techniques*, p. 80, for cable cast-on and twisted cord. **2** For Large Bag, MC = A, CC = B; for Small Bag, MC = B, CC = A.

K1 under strand

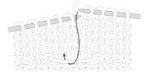

1 Take the tip of the right-hand needle under the strand created by slipping the stitches on Row 2.

2 Knit next stitch on left-hand needle.

3 Pass the strand over the stitch just knit.

LARGE BAG

With 2 strands CC held together, cast on 53 sts tightly over 2 needles. Remove 1 needle and cut 1 strand of CC. Knit 1 row with single strand. Cut yarn.

Shape flap

Row 1 (WS) Sl 12 sts to right-hand needle, then join MC and k5, [p7, k5] 2 times, p1, turn work, leaving remaining 11 sts unworked.
Row 2 Join CC and k6, [sl 7 wyif, k5] 2 times, k1, turn work.
Row 3 P1, k5, [p7, k5] 2 times, p2, turn work.
Row 4 With MC, k33, turn work.
Row 5 P2, k5, [p7, k5] 2 times, p3, turn work.
Row 6 With MC, [k11, k1 under strand] 2 times, k11, turn work.

Row 7 P3, k5, p7, bind off 4 sts for slot for bag tab (1 st remaining on right-hand needle after bind-off), p7, k5, p4, turn work.

Row 8 With CC, k9, sl 7 wyif, bring yarn to back of work, sl 1 from right-hand needle to left-hand needle, bring yarn to front again, sl st back to right-hand needle, bring yarn to back and k1, turn work and cable cast on 4 sts onto left-hand needle, turn work, sl 1 wyif, bring yarn to back of work, replace slipped st, bring yarn to front and sl 7, k9, turn work.

Row 9 P4, k5, [p7, k5] 2 times, p5, turn work.

Row 10 With MC, k39, turn work.

Row 11 P5, k5, [p7, k5] 2 times, p6, turn work.

Row 12 With MC, k14, k1 under strand, k11, k1 under strand, k14, turn work.

Row 13 P6, k5, [p7, k5] 2 times, p7, turn work.

Row 14 With CC, k12, [sl 7 wyif, k5] 2 times, k7, turn work.

Row 15 [P7, k5] 3 times, p8, turn work.

Row 16 With MC, k45, turn work.

Row 17 K1, [p7, k5] 3 times, p7, k2, turn work.

Row 18 With MC, k17, [k1 under strand, k11] 2 times, k6, turn work.

Row 19 K2, [p7, k5] 3 times, p7, k3, turn work.

Row 20 With CC, K3, [sl 7 wyif, k5] 3 times, sl 7 wyif, k3, turn work.

HIMALAYA YARN COMPANY Recycled Silk (100% silk; 3½oz/100g; 80yds/73m) Multicolor (A) and Handspun Silk (100% silk; 3½oz/100g; 180yds/ 164m) Black (B)

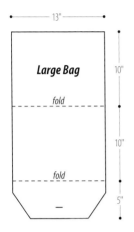

Large Bag

13"

fold

fold

10"

10"

5"

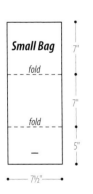

Small Bag

fold

fold

7"

7"

5"

7½"

Row 21 K3, [p7, k5] 3 times, p7, k4, turn work.
Row 22 With MC, k51, turn work.
Row 23 K4, [p7, k5] 4 times.
Row 24 With MC, k8, [k1 under strand, k11] 3 times, k1 under strand, k8.
Work 6 rows of Pattern St 22 times, then work Row 1 once more. Bind off with CC.

Finishing
Block piece to measurements. Fold bag as shown and sew side seams. With CC, make a twisted cord approximately 36" long and attach to inside of each side.

Tab
With CC, cast on 6 sts. Work 2½" in garter st (knit every row). Bind off. Attach long strands of fringe along bound-off edge. Knot beads into fringe. End by knotting all fringe ends together (the large knot makes it easier to manipulate the tab through the slot). Attach tab to front of bag to correspond to slot on flap.

Optional lining
The lining will need to be a bit smaller than the dimensions of the bag. This ease is provided by omitting seam allowances when cutting the lining. From lining fabric, cut a strip twice the width of the bag by twice the height. With right sides together, sew a ½" seam along the edge that represents the height measurement. Press the seam open. Fold the tube in half, matching the seam

allowances on the inside. Press the fold. Cut a strip of heavy interfacing twice the width of the bag by the height, less ½". Overlap the short edge by 1", and sew a line of stitching down the center of the overlapped edges. Trim away extra interfacing on either side of stitching. Slip the interfacing tube between the lining layers, matching edge of interfacing to fold in top of lining, and matching seams. Press flat, with the seam down the center back. Sew ½" seam along the bottom. Trim seam allowance. Tuck into bag with raw seam allowance facing down.

Twisted cord
1 Cut strands 6 times the length of cord needed. Fold in half and knot the cut ends together.
2 With knotted end in left hand and right index finger in folded end, twist clockwise until cord is tightly twisted.
3 Fold cord in half and smooth as it twists on itself; knot.

SMALL BAG

With 2 strands CC, cast on 29 sts tightly over 2 needles. Remove 1 needle and cut 1 strand of CC. Knit 1 row with single strand. Work 6 rows of Pattern St.

Next row (WS) With MC, k5, p7, bind off 4 sts for Tab (1 st remaining on right-hand needle after bind-off), p7, k5.

Next row With CC, k5, sl 7 wyif, bring yarn to back of work, slip 1 from right-hand needle to left-hand needle, bring yarn to front again, sl st back to right-hand needle, bring yarn to back and k1, turn work and cable cast on 4 sts onto left-hand needle, turn work, sl 1 wyif, bring yarn to back of work, replace slipped st, bring yarn to front and sl 7, k5. Work Rows 3–6 of Pattern Stitch once, then work Rows 1–6 of Pattern Stitch 18 times. Work Row 1 once more. Bind off with MC.

Finishing

Block piece to measurements. Fold bag as shown and sew side seams. With MC, make a twisted cord approximately 30" long and attach to inside of each side. Make Tab as for large bag.

Just as special things happen when the planets align, special patterns happen when colors align as you knit circularly with variegated yarn. The results can be bold and dramatic or subtle and fluid.

Designed by Jane Davis

Zigzag Bags

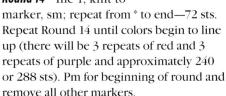

EASY

34" circumference x 11 ½" high
• approximate measurements

10cm/4"

36

28
• over stockinette st (knit all rounds)
• approximate, adjust if necessary to maintain color stacking (see p. 47)

1 2 3 **4** 5 6

• Medium weight
• 570 yds

• 4mm/US6, or size to obtain gauge, 40cm and 60cm (16" and 24") long

• 4.5 mm/US7 double-pointed needles (dpn)

&

• Stitch markers

Notes

1 See *Techniques*, p. 80, for crochet cast-on, I-cord, grafting, and grafting open sts to cast-on edge. **2** Read Stacking with Multi-colored Yarns, p. 47. **3** Change to circular needle (or longer circular needle) when necessary.

LARGE RAINBOW BAG

With dpns, cast on 3 sts. Divided evenly over 3 dpns, join, and work in rounds as follows:

Round 1 [Knit into front and back of next st (Inc 1)] 3 times—6 sts.

Round 2 [Inc 1] 6 times—12 sts.

Round 3 [Inc 1, k1, place marker (pm), Inc 1, k1] 3 times—18 sts.

Round 4 [Inc 1, knit to marker, sl marker (sm), Inc 1, knit to end of needle] 3 times—24 sts.

Round 5 Repeat Round 4—30 sts.

Round 6 Knit.

Rounds 7–11 [Repeat Round 4] 5 times—60 sts.

Round 12 Knit.

Round 13 With 16" circular needle, work sts from dpns as follows: Inc 1, knit to marker, sm, Inc 1, knit to end of needle, pm] 3 times—66 sts.

Round 14 * Inc 1, knit to marker, sm; repeat from * to end—72 sts. Repeat Round 14 until colors begin to line up (there will be 3 repeats of red and 3 repeats of purple and approximately 240 or 288 sts). Pm for beginning of round and remove all other markers.

Continue working in St st until piece measures 10" from last increase round.

Next round Increase or decrease sts (depending on your current st count) evenly around so that the total number of sts is either 240 or 288, whichever number is closer to your stitch count.

Top border

Work 2 rounds in k2, p2 rib.

Eyelet round * [K2, p2] twice, k2, p1, yarn over (yo) twice, p1; repeat from * to end—280 or 336 sts.

Next round * [K2, p2] 3 times, p1 through back loop, p1; repeat from * to end of round.

Next round * [K2, p2] twice, k2, p2tog 2 times; repeat from * to end—240 or 288 sts.

Work 1" in k2, p2 rib. Bind off in pattern.

Finishing
I-cord

Cast on 5 sts. Work 5-st I-cord for 108". Do not bind off. Clamp cast-on end to a stationary surface and holding working end, twist cord until it kinks up. Fold the cord in half and help it twist around itself smoothly. Clamp the cast-on and working ends together so they don't lose the twist. Take folded end and weave it in and out of eyelets in the ribbing on the bag. Unclamp the ends of the I-cord and run the cast-on end through the loop at the folded end, then graft the open sts to the cast-on sts (see illustration).

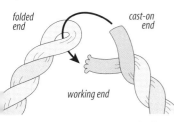

Run cast-on end through loop at folded end and graft open stitches to cast-on stitches.

LORNA'S LACES Bullfrogs and Butterflies (85% wool/15% mohair; 4oz/125g; 190yds/173m) was used in all bags unless otherwise noted.

EASY

6½"–8½" wide x 5" high
• approximate measurements

10cm/4"

32–36

24–28
• over stockinette st (knit all rounds)
• approximate, adjust if necessary to maintain color stacking (see p. 47)

1 2 **3-4** 5 6
• Light–Medium weight
• 150 yds

• 3.5mm– 4.5mm/US4–7, or size to obtain gauge, double-pointed needles (dpn)

&

• Stitch markers, 7–9" zipper, beads for zipper pull, needle and thread

Dark bag: TAHKI Cotton Classic (100% cotton; 1¾oz/50g; 108yds/98m)

SMALL NOTIONS BAG

Work Rounds 1–6 as for Large Rainbow Bag.
Then, repeat Round 4 until the colors begin to line up. Place marker for beginning of round, removing all other markers. Work even until piece measures 5" from beginning. Bind off.

Finishing

Fold bag and press flat. Sew zipper in opening (see p. 21). Sew beads to zipper pull. Make a 5-st I-cord 10" long and sew one end to top of bag at base of zipper. Work as I-cord for Large Rainbow Bag.

EASY

18" wide x 5" high
• approximate measurements

10cm/4"
24
18
• over stockinette st (knit all rounds)
• approximate, adjust if necessary to
maintain color stacking (see page 47)

1 2 3 **4** 5 6

• Medium weight
• 300 yds

• 4.5mm/US7, or size to obtain gauge,
60cm (24") long

&

• Stitch markers, 18" zipper, beads for
zipper pull, thread and needle

LONG BAG

Crochet cast on approximately 170 sts (must be an even number), adjusting cast-on as necessary to get colors to line up (see p. 47; there will be two complete repeats of the color pattern). Join and work in St st (knit every round) until piece measures 5" from beginning. Fold tube and graft half the sts to the other half to close one side. Sew an 18" zipper in opening on other side (p. 21), stitching excess ends of opening together.

Strap

Cast on 6 sts. Work 10" in Seed st. Bind off. Sew strap to one end of bag. Attach beads to zipper pull.

LIBERTY BAG

Seed St

Row/Round 1 * K1, p1; repeat from *.
Row/Round 2 Knit the purl sts and purl
the knit sts.
Repeat Row/Round 2 for Seed st.

Work Rounds 1–6 as for Large Rainbow
Bag. Repeat Round 4 until colors begin
to line up. Place marker at beginning of
round, removing all other markers. Work
even until piece measures 8" from last
increase round, increase or decrease
evenly (if necessary) on last round to a
number divisible by 4. Work 3 rounds of
Seed st.

Flap

Next round Bind off half the sts and work
in Seed st to end. Work Seed st back
and forth in rows on remaining sts for
1". Continuing in pattern, decrease 1 st
each side every row until 4 sts remain.
Work 4-st I-cord for 2½". Loop end to
beginning of I-cord and sew in place.

I-cord Strap

Cast on 5 sts. Work 5-st I-cord for 32".
Bind off. Sew ends of I-cord to back of
bag at each side, below Seed St. Sew a
large hanging bead to center of bag front
for a closure.

STACKING MULTICOLORED YARNS

The colors in a variegated yarn can produce an interesting vertical pattern. Either machine-dyed or hand-dyed yarns may be used, as long as the yarn has regular intervals of color.

The exact number of stitches to work for each round is determined by the color repeat of the yarn, stitch tension, and needle size. Start with a small circle on double-pointed needles and increase round by round until the colors line up with those of the previous round. To maintain this stacking pattern, knit around without increasing (forming a closed-end tube).

The size of your tube is determined by the number of repeats of the color pattern in each round. For our smallest bag, use a single repeat (stop increasing and knit even the first time you see the colors align). For a larger bag, continue increasing after you see the first color alignment. The colors will move out of alignment, then when there are enough stitches, the colors will re-align and each round will contain two repeats of the color pattern. Of course, more repeats can be added for larger tubes.

The Long Bag requires all stitches (the full circumference) to be cast on. But first you have to understand the yarn's color repeat. Reel off a few yards of yarn. Wind the yarn in a ring, adjusting the size of the ring until the colors align on top of one another.

Now check to see what you've got. Take note of the exact length of the repeat. Tie a small strand of smooth, contrasting yarn at the end of every repeat for the first few yards. Cast on into a crochet chain of smooth, contrasting-color yarn (make the chain much longer than you think you'll need (see *Techniques*, p. 80, for crochet cast-on). Cast on stitches into the chain, consuming the entire length of the first repeat. (Remember a repeat is from marker to marker.) Now begin your Long Bag, casting on the multiple of the repeat that is closest to the stitch number called for in the instructions.

As you knit, the colors will shift slightly, but you can influence the direction by the way you knit. To make the stripes slant to the left, knit tight for a few stitches by wrapping the yarn around your finger twice or changing which hand holds the yarn or even decreasing a stitch or two. To slant the colors to the right, knit loosely or increase. In either case, after a few stitches, restore normal tension or number of stitches.

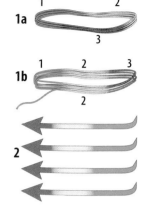

1a Linear or sequential pattern in multi-colored yarn

1b Undulating pattern in multi-colored yarn

2 Circular knitting with linear and undulating color sequences

Mitered knitting plus felting equals attractive, clever, and useful accessories made from simple squares and strips in garter stitch. Choosing your color scheme may be more difficult than the knitting.

Designed by Joan McGowan-Michael

Four-Square Mitered Tote

INTERMEDIATE

12" wide (at widest point) x 8" high x 3½ " deep, after felting

10cm/4"

32
16
• over garter stitch (knit every row), before felting

1 2 **3** 4 5 6

• Light weight
A • 214 yds
B, C, D, E • 107 yds each

• 5.5mm/US9, or size to obtain gauge

• 5.5mm/US9, 60mm (24") long

&

• One button 1¾"/32mm
• Yarn needle

69-row Stripe Pattern

Rows	Color	Rows	Color
4 rows	B	4 rows	D
2 rows	A	2 rows	E
2 rows	D	4 rows	B
6 rows	C	6 rows	C
4 rows	E	2 rows	D
2 rows	B	4 rows	A
4 rows	C	4 rows	E
6 rows	A	13 rows	B

Square (make 8)

With B, cast on 71 sts. Work 69-row Stripe Pattern. AT SAME TIME, work shaping as follows: *Row 1* (RS) K34, k3tog, k34. *2 and all WS rows* Knit. *Row 3* K33, k3tog, k33. Continue working 1 fewer knit st at each side of center k3tog on every RS row until 3 sts remain, end with Pattern Row 68. *Row 69* K3tog. Fasten off last st.

Gusset

Note Work Stripe pattern of gusset randomly, changing color as desired, leaving enough color A to work strap. Cast on 30 sts. Work in garter st until piece measures 48". Bind off.

Finishing

Sew 4 squares together, matching cast-on edges, for bag front and back. Sew gusset onto side panels (see illustration).

TOP BORDER

With RS facing, circular needle, and A, pick up and knit 200 sts evenly around top of bag. Join and knit 3 rounds, purl 1 round (for turning ridge), knit 3 rounds. Bind off. Turn border to WS at turning ridge and sew in place.

Straps (make 2)

With A, cast on 10 sts. Work in St st (k on RS, p on WS) for 200 rows. Bind off.

Felting

Felt bag and straps as instructed on p. 7. Block by inserting appropriately sized cardboard box inside wet bag, let dry. Using photo as guide, sew straps to each side of bag, angling bottom of strap to match 45 degree angle of stripes.

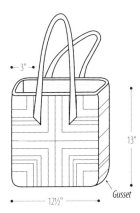

3"

13"

12½"

Gusset

JO SHARP 100% Pure Wool (100% wool;
1.75oz/50g; 107yds/98m) Gray (A), Red (B),
Blue (C), Light Blue (D), and Ivory (E)

"This tote bag is so easy to use! The drawstring opens easily when you set it down and it closes itself when you pick it up—a boon for people like me, who are usually in a hurry and can forget to close a bag!"

Designed by Susanna Lewis

It's in the Bag

EASY +

14" wide x 16" long

10cm/4"

46

32

• over stockinette stitch approximate; use stitch size 6–8, and wash and dry swatch

 2 3 4 5 6

• Super Fine weight
MC • 1200 yds
CC1, CC2, CC3 • 100 yds each

Standard gauge, single-bed knitting machine

&

• 10 grommets
• 2 yds cotton cording to fit through grommets

MACHINE KNITTING INSTRUCTIONS

Tuck-stitch beading

(2 rows) Bring every other needle to holding position, carriage set for hold. With next color, knit 2 rows (working position needles knit 2 rows, holding position needles have 2 loops over the needle stem). Set carriage to knit all stitches, change to next color, and proceed to next stripe.

Stripe Pattern

NUMBER OF ROWS — COLORS USED

	Rep 1	Rep 2	Rep 3
2 in beading	CC1	CC2	CC3
2 in St st	MC	MC	MC
4 in St st	CC2	CC3	CC1
2 in beading	CC3	CC1	CC2
2 in St st	CC2	CC3	CC1
6 in St st	CC1	CC2	CC3
10 in St st	MC	MC	MC

Total 26 rows each repeat.

Notes 1 See *Techniques*, p. 80, for mattress stitch and single crochet. **2** The bag is knit in stockinette stitch (St st) throughout, and decorated with rows of tuck-stitch beading. The beading adds rows to row count (RC) but no length to knitting.

Outside of bag

With waste yarn, cast on 108 sts and knit some rows. Change to MC. Knit 9 rows, then make an eyelet on 8th needle from right selvedge, by transferring its stitch to next needle either side. Leave empty needle in working position. Knit 18 rows in MC. Set RC000. Begin Stripe Pattern by referring to listing for colors to use for each of 3 repeats of Stripe Pattern. Knit 6 complete repeats, RC=168. Finish by knitting 2 rows beading in CC1, 2 rows MC, 4 rows CC2, then make 4 eyelets: skip 13 needles, transfer next stitch to either side, * skip 26 needles, make eyelet on next needle; repeat from * 3 times more. Knit 4 more rows CC2, 4 rows MC, 2 rows beading in CC3. Leave stitches on needles and continue with lining.

Lining

Knit in St st with MC. Set carriage to knit all sts, knit 2 rows. Decrease 1 st each side. Knit 2 rows, then hang a hem by putting sts from uppermost CC2 row below onto same needles. Knit 4 rows, make 4 eyelets on same needles as before. Knit 4 more rows, hang another hem by putting sts from uppermost MC row below onto same needles. Set RC000 and knit straight for

163 rows. Make an eyelet on 8th needle from right selvedge. Knit 9 more rows. Knit several rows waste yarn and remove piece from machine. Knit 2nd piece the same, the only change being placement of first and last eyelets. Place them on 8th needle from left selvedge.

Finishing

Sew sides of 2 pieces together with mattress stitch, from the RS. Single crochet (sc) across bottom of outside of bag from WS (turn bag inside out). Be sure all yarn ends are knotted, then sc across bottom of lining, from RS. Push lining inside bag. Install grommets through both layers of fabric.

Cord

With MC, cast on 4 sts. Set carriage to knit in one direction, slip or free pass other direction. Knit about 2 yds of cord. Thread cotton cording through it and finish ends. Wash and dry bag, then thread cord through eyelets as shown in sketch on p. 53 and knot ends.

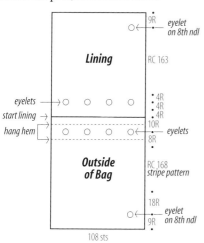

GALLER YARNS *Parisian Cotton* (100% mercerized cotton; 1oz/28g; 120yds/109m)

14" wide x 17" high
before washing

10cm/4"

28
20
• over stockinette stitch
(knit all rounds)
before washing

1 2 **3** 4 5 6

• Light weight
MC, A, B • 204 yds each
C • 125 yds

• 3.75mm/US5, or size to obtain gauge,
40cm (16") long

&

• 10 grommets, with a ¼" hole
• one extra 3.75/US5 needle for 3-needle
bind-off

HANDKNIT VARIATION
Notes
1 See *Techniques*, p. 80, for 3-needle bind-off, I-cord, and yo. *2* Slip sts purlwise with yarn to WS.

Pattern 1
Rounds 1, 2 With C, * sl 1, k1, repeat from * to end.
Rounds 3, 4 With MC, work in St st.
Rounds 5–8 With A, work in St st.
Rounds 9, 10 With C * sl 1, k1, repeat from * to end.
Rounds 11, 12 With B, work in St st.
Rounds 13–18 With MC, work in St st.
Rounds 19–28 With A, work in St st.

Pattern 2
Rounds 1, 2 With C, * sl 1, k1, repeat from * to end.
Rounds 3, 4 With B, work in St st.
Rounds 5–8 With MC, work in St st.
Rounds 9, 10 With C, * sl 1, k1, repeat from * to end.
Rounds 11, 12 With A, work in St st.
Rounds 13–18 With B, work in St st.
Rounds 19–28 With MC, work in St st.

Pattern 3
Rounds 1, 2 With C, * sl 1, k1, repeat from * to end.
Rounds 3, 4 With A, work in St st.
Rounds 5–8 With B, work in St st.

Rounds 9, 10 With C, * sl 1, k1, repeat from * to end.
Rounds 11, 12 With MC, work in St st.
Rounds 13–18 With A, work in St st.
Rounds 19–28 With B, work in St st.

BAG
Picot edge
With A, cast on 140 sts. Place marker to indicate the beginning of the round. Work 4 rounds in stockinette stitch (St st; knit every round).
Next round * Yo, k2tog * around.
Work 5 rounds in St st.
Work Rounds 1-6 of Pattern 1.
Round 7 (Grommet Preparation Row) Maintaining Pattern 1, k4, yo twice, k2tog, [k19, yo twice, k2tog] three times, k9, yo twice, k2tog, [k19, yo twice, k2tog] twice, k12, yo twice, k2tog, knit to end.
Round 8 Maintaining Pattern 1, knit only the first wrap of the yo's, dropping the second off of the needle.
Continue Pattern 1, then work Pattern 2 and 3. Repeat Pattern 1.
Work Rounds 1 and 2 of Pattern 2.
Round 3 Maintaining Pattern 2, k4, yo twice, k2tog, knit to last 6 sts, yo twice, k2tog, knit to end.
Round 4 Maintaining Pattern 2, knit only the first wrap of the yo, dropping the second off of the needle.

Finishing

Turn bag inside out and work 3-needle bind-off to seam the bottom of the bag. Fasten off. Whipstitch cast–on edge to Round 10 of the Picot edge. Weave in ends. Insert grommets at designated spots.

Strap

With C, cast on 4 sts and work I-cord for 2 yds. Weave through grommets and tie in a knot as illustrated below.

Pick it up here and carry like a shopping bag.

Pick it up here and carry on one shoulder.

ROWAN Denim (100% cotton; 1¾oz/50g; 102 yds/93m)

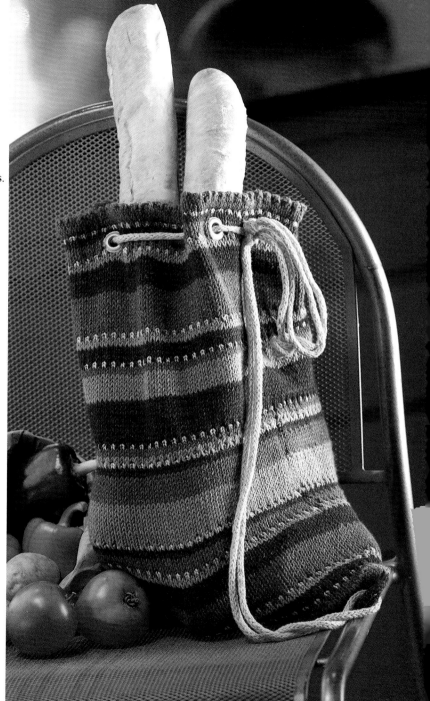

This sweater-backpack duo is ideal for cooler summer days at the shore or for early fall wearing. The sturdy backpack is formed from two uncomplicated fabric-like stitches.

Designed by Cynthia Helene

Season-Spanners Duo

INTERMEDIATE

30¾" circumference x 17" high

10cm/4"

28

24

• over Main Pattern Stitch
using 5mm/US8 needles

1 2 3 **4** 5 6

• Medium weight
A & B • 300 yds each
C & D • 200 yds each

• 5mm/US8, or size to obtain gauge,
60cm (24") long
• 4.5 and 5.5mm/US7 and 9, 60cm (24") long

• 4.5mm/US7 double-pointed needle (dpn)
• Two 5.5mm/US9 dpn for I-cord.

• 1 toggle button

BACKPACK
Notes
1 See *Techniques,* p. 80, for I-cord.
2 Work bag back and forth on circular needles. **3** Work Backpack Chart in intarsia technique (see p. 57).

Main Pattern Stitch
Row 1 (RS) * Knit into back of second st on left-hand needle, then knit first st, slipping both sts off needle at the same time (1/1LC); repeat from *.
Row 2 Purl.
Row 3 K1, * 1/1LC; repeat from * to last st, k1.
Row 4 Purl.
Repeat Rows 1–4 for Main Pattern Stitch.
Linen stitch
Row 1 (RS) * K1, slip 1 (sl 1) with yarn in front; repeat from * to last 2 sts, k2.
Row 2 * P1, sl1 with yarn in back; repeat from * to last 2 sts, p2.

Repeat Rows 1 and 2 for Linen Stitch.
Main Piece
With 5mm/US8 circular needle, cast on 184 sts and begin working in Main Pattern Stitch from Backpack chart as follows:
Row 1 (RS) Work 20 sts with color B, 26 sts with A, 28 sts with B, 46 sts with A, 22 sts with C, 42 sts with D.
Row 2 Purl in established colors.
Row 3 (RS) Work 21 sts with B, 26 sts with A, 28 sts with B, 46 sts with A, 22 sts with C, 41 sts with D.
Row 4 Purl in established colors.
Continue working in this manner through Row 108.
Eyelets
Row 109 Work 8 sts, * bind off 2 sts; with 1 st already on the RH needle, work 8 more sts; repeat from * to last 11 sts, bind off 2 sts, work to end.
Row 110 Purl across casting on 2 sts over each pair of bound-off sts from previous row. Work 10 rows even. Bind off.
Base
With 5.5mm/US9 needle and B, cast on 22 sts and work in Linen Stitch until Base measures 11¾", ending with Row 2. Bind off.

54

Straps (make 2)

With largest needles and A, cast on 10 sts and work in Linen Stitch until work measures 25½" or desired length, ending with a WS row. Bind off.

Flap

Color sequence 10 rows B, 8 rows C, 26 rows B, 12 rows C, 24 rows B, 12 rows C, 8 rows B.

With largest circular needle and B, cast on 40 sts. Work in Linen Stitch in color sequence, AT SAME TIME, when piece measures 8", end with Row 2.

* *Next row* P1, p2tog, work to last 3 sts, p2tog, p1.
Next row Work across. *

Repeat from * to * 3 times more.

Next row P1, p2tog, work 11 sts, bind off 4 sts, work to last 3 sts, p2tog, p1.

Next row Work to end, casting on 4 sts over bound-off sts from previous row.

Repeat from * to * 3 times more. Bind off remaining 24 sts in pattern.

Drawstring

With dpn and D, cast on 4 sts and make 43¼" I-cord (see *Techniques*, p. 80). Bind off.

Flap edging

With WS facing, using 4.5/US7 needle and D, pick up and knit 30 sts across cast-on edge, 49 sts along side edge, 18 sts across bound-off edge, and 49 sts along remaining side edge—146 sts. Work in St st (k on RS, p on WS) for 7 rows, beginning with a knit row. Bind off purlwise, working p2tog at corners to retain shape of hem. Sew edge seam. Stitch bound-off edge of edging to RS of flap.

CYNTHIA HELENE Merino 12 ply (100% wool; 1¾oz/50g; 99yds/90m) Beige (A), Gray (B), Blue (C), and Camel (D)

Backpack chart

B 11–12 sts	C R 101: 30 sts	A	B R 95	C R 103: 42 sts	A	B R 101
	20 sts	R 87: 22 sts		18 sts	R 95: 36 sts	
D R 61		B R 65: 42 sts	D R 57	A R 75	D R 71	A
	B R 49		C R 45	B R 57	C R 39	R 51
C 22 sts	C R 21: 20 sts	A R 33	B 22 sts	A R 17: 24 sts	D R 23	B
	D R 1: 42–41 sts	C 22 sts	46 sts	B 28 sts	A 26 sts	20–21 sts

184 sts

Finishing

Fold Main Piece in half lengthwise and sew side edges together to form center back seam. With center back seam and WS of straps facing, slip stitch ends of straps to main piece 1½" in from side edges at lower corners. Sew Base in position, taking care to stitch straps firmly in place. Place center of Flap to back seam and sew cast-on edge in position just below eyelets.

Taking care not to twist Straps, sew remaining ends firmly in position just below cast-on edge on Flap, placing inner edges together at center back seam. Beginning at center back seam, thread one end of Drawstring through eyelets around to center front. Thread remaining end to match, tying at center front. Sew on button to correspond with buttonhole.

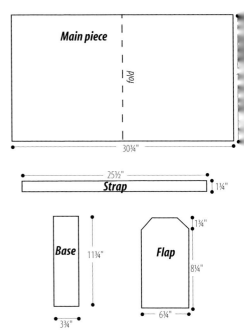

Main piece

fold

30¾"

Strap

25½"

1¾"

Base

11¾"

3¾"

Flap

1¾"

8¼"

6¾"

INTARSIA

When changing from one color to the next when working intarsia, it is necessary to twist the yarns to prevent holes. Pick up the new color from under the old color, as shown, and continue working.

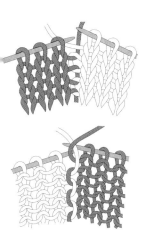

Season-Spanners Duo

EASY +

C

B | A

LOOSE FIT

S (M, L)
A 44 (48, 52)"
B 20 (20½, 21)"
C 28 (29¼, 30¾)"

10cm/4"

24

18
• over stockinette stitch
(knit on RS, purl on WS)
using smaller needles

10cm/4"

20

16
• over Twisted Rib using both sizes
of needles

1 2 3 **4** 5 6

• Medium weight
• 890 (990, 1090) yds

• 5 and 8mm/US8 and 11,
or size to obtain gauge

• 5mm/US8, 40cm (16") long

SWEATER

Twisted Rib OVER AN EVEN NUMBER OF STS

Row 1 (RS) With larger needles, sl 1, p1, * k1 through back loop p1; repeat from * to end.
Row 2 With smaller needles, * k1, p1; repeat from * to end.
Repeat Rows 1 and 2 for Twisted Rib.

Back

With smaller needles, cast on 88 (96, 104) sts.
Purl 4 rows.
Work in Twisted Rib until piece measures 20 (20½, 21)" from beginning, ending with a WS row. With smaller needle, bind off.

Front

Work as for Back until piece measures 17 (17¼, 17¾)" from beginning, ending with a WS row.

Shape neck

Next row Work 39 (43, 46) sts, join 2nd ball of yarn, bind off center 10 (10, 12) sts, work to end. Working both sides at same time, decrease 1 st at neck edge every row 9 (10, 10) times. Work even until piece measures same length as Back to shoulders. Bind off remaining 30 (33, 36) sts.

Sleeves

With smaller needles, cast on 46 sts. Purl 4 rows. Work in Pattern stitch, AT SAME TIME, increase 1 st each side every 6th row 8 (12, 12) times, then every 8th (8th, 4th) row 4 (1, 2) times—70 (72, 74) sts. Work even until Sleeve measures 17" from beginning, end with a WS row. Using larger needle, bind off in pattern.

Finishing

Block pieces. Sew shoulder seams. Mark a point 9 (9¼, 9½)" down from shoulder on sides of Back and Front for armholes. Sew Sleeves between markers. Sew side and Sleeve seams.

Neckband

With RS facing, using smaller circular needle, pick up and k18 sts down Left Front neck, 10 (10, 12) sts across center Front, 18 sts up Right Front neck and 28 (30, 32) sts across center Back—74 (76, 80) sts. Purl 1 row. Knit 1 row. Purl 1 row. Bind off.

7 (7½, 8)" 7½ (8¼, 9)"

Front

Back

3 (3¼, 3¾)"

17 (17¼, 17¾)"

9 (9¼, 9½)"

11 (11¼, 11½)"

22 (24, 26)"

17½ (18, 18½)"

Sleeve

17"

11½"

Knitting a sturdy, versatile bag doesn't have to involve rugged yarns and firm gauge. Felting gives this backpack added durability. With two sizes, there's a pack for every back.

Designed by Linda Cyr

Fabulous Felted Backpacks

INTERMEDIATE

Child's
7" high x 11" wide x 5" deep
Adult's
10" high x 12" wide x 6" deep,
after felting

10cm/4"

20

12
• over stockinette stitch
(knit on RS, purl on WS)

1 2 3 4 **5** 6

• Bulky weight
• 375 yds for adult's
• 300 yds for child's

• 6mm/US10, or size to obtain gauge

&

• Cable needle (cn)

Notes
1 See *Techniques*, p. 80, for I-cord.
2 Backpack body is worked first, then base is added.

BACKPACK
Body
Cast on 99 (123) sts.
Begin Charts
Row 1 (RS) Work 12 (16) sts Chart A, 4 sts Chart B, 16 (20) sts Chart A, 4 sts Chart B, p0 (2), 8 sts Chart C, p0 (2), 11 sts Chart D, p0 (2), 8 sts Chart C, p0 (2), 4 sts Chart E, 16 (20) sts Chart A, 4 sts Chart E, 12 (16) sts Chart A.
Row 2 (WS) Work 12 (16) sts Chart A, 4 sts Chart E, 16 (20) sts Chart A, 4 sts Chart E, k0 (2), 8 sts Chart C, k0 (2), 11 sts Chart D, k0 (2), 8 sts Chart C, k0 (2), 4 sts Chart B, 16 (20) sts Chart A, 4 sts Chart B, 12 (16) sts Chart A.
Continue patterns as established until 8 rows of charts have been worked 6 (7) times, then work Rows 1 and 2 once more.

Vertical eyelet band
Knit 4 rows. Work vertical eyelets:
Next row (RS) K5 (6), turn work.
Next row (WS) K5 (6), turn work.

Repeat last 2 rows once more.
Next row (RS) K5 (6), yo twice, k8 (10), turn work.
* **Next row** K7 (9), k2tog, turn work.
Next row (RS) K8 (10), turn work.
Next row K7 (9), k2tog, turn work.
Next row K8 (10), yo twice, k8 (10), turn work. *
Repeat from * to * 4 times more, ending last repeat k9 (11) instead of k8 (10), turn work.
Next row (RS) K8 (10), k2tog, turn work.
Next row K9 (11), turn work.
Next row K8 (10), k2tog, turn work.
Next row K9 (11), yo twice, k8 (10), turn work.
Work from * to * 5 times, ending last repeat k5 (6), turn work.
Next 4 rows K5 (6), turn work.
Knit 5 rows over all sts. Bind off.

Base
Cast on 28 (36) sts. Work Chart A for 30 (42) rows, end with Chart Row 6 (2). Bind off.

Drawstring strap
Make one 4-yd (5-yd) length of 4-st I-cord. Bind off.

K on RS, p on WS

P on RS, k on WS

1/1 RC K2tog, leaving sts on left-hand needle, then knit first st; drop both sts from needle

1/1 LC With right-hand needle behind work, knit 2nd st on left-hand needle through back loop, then knit first st through front loop; drop both sts from needle

2 RC Sl 2 to cn, hold to back, k2; k2 from cn

2/2 LC Sl 2 to cn, hold to front, k2; k2 from cn

2/2/2 KC Sl 4 to cn, hold to front, k2; sl 2 sts from cn to LH needle, hold cn to back, p2 from LH needle; k2 from cn

B Make Bobble [(K1, p1) twice, k1] in next st, turn, p5; sl 2nd, 3rd, 4th and 5th sts, one at a time, over first st and off needle

BROWN SHEEP COMPANY Lamb's Pride Bulky (85% wool, 15% mohair; 4 oz/113g; 125yds/114m)

Chart A

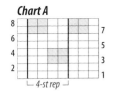

└ 4-st rep ┘

Chart B

4 sts

Chart C

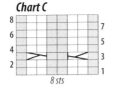

8 sts

Chart D

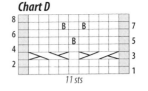

11 sts

Chart E

4 sts

Pattern Arrangement

Chart A	Chart E	Chart A	Chart E	Rev St st	Chart C	Rev St st	Chart D	Rev St st	Chart C	Rev St st	Chart B	Chart A	Chart B	Chart A
12 (16) sts	4 sts	16 (20) sts	4 sts	0 (2) sts	8 sts	0 (2) sts	11 sts	0 (2) sts	8 sts	0 (2) sts	4 sts	16 (20) sts	4 sts	12 (16) sts

61

Finishing

Felt all pieces (see p. 7). Steam block all pieces. Sew back seam of body. Sew base to 4 sides of body. Find center of strap and attach it to center front of base. Sew strap along front and 2 sides (see illustration). Take left side of strap and thread it through eyelet nearest front on left side of backpack (shown by arrow). Go out next eyelet to right (first eyelet of front), then in and out until cord comes out remaining eyelet on left side of backpack. Repeat for right side of strap, working in opposite direction around backpack, and keeping strap on top of first strap. Sew ends of strap together. Attach the join to center back of base. Sew straps down to each side of base, taking a few extra stitches at 2 corners through both straps.

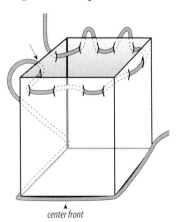

center front

17

Combine a rustic wool yarn and some great stitches to make this useful bag. Details that include a built-in I-cord edging and front-button closure give a tailored finish—the easy way.

Designed by Edie Eckman

Aran Pocketbook

INTERMEDIATE

10" wide x 8" high x 2" deep

10cm/4"

26

13

• over garter st (knit every row)

1 2 3 4 **5** 6

• Bulky weight
• 250 yds

• 5.5mm/US9, or size to obtain gauge

• One 1"/25mm

&

• Cable needle (cn), stitch holders
• Lining material and matching sewing thread (optional)

Notes
1 See *Techniques*, p. 80, for grafting.
2 Slip sts purlwise with yarn in back unless specified otherwise.

POCKETBOOK
Cast on 40 sts. Purl 4 rows. Work Rows 1–41 of Chart Pattern (front). Purl 8 rows (base). Work Rows 12–52 of Chart Pattern (back).
Shape flap
Next row (WS) Purl to last 3 sts, sl 3. Repeat last row 7 times more.
Decrease row P4, p2tog, purl to last 3 sts, sl 3.
Repeat Decrease Row until 8 sts remain.
Next row (WS) P3, p2tog, sl 3.
Next row P4, place remaining 3 sts on hold. Do not turn. Return 4 sts to left-hand needle, p2, p2tog—3 sts. [Return sts to left-hand needle, p3] 6 times. Graft open sts to sts on hold, forming button loop.
Strap
Note Strap also forms sides of pocketbook.
Cast on 9 sts.
Row 1 K6, sl 3 sts purlwise with yarn in front.

Repeat Row 1 until strap measures 46". Bind off.
Finishing
Line bag (see p. 40). Fold front and back of pocketbook up. Sew each end of strap along 8 rows of base. Sew edges of strap along sides of bag. Sew button on front.

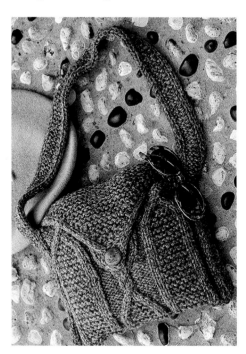

Legend

☐	K on RS, p on WS
▨	P on RS, k on WS
⟍⟍	**2/1 RPC** Sl 1 to cn, hold to back, k2; p1 from cn
⟍⟍	**2/1 LPC** Sl 2 to cn, hold to front, p1; k2 from cn
⟍⟍	**2/2 RC** Sl 2 to cn, hold to back, k2; k2 from cn

Chart Pattern

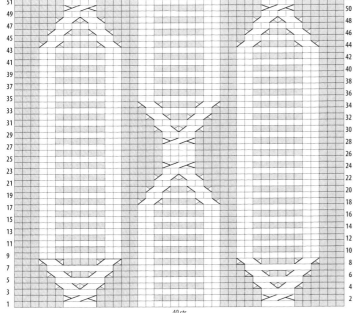

40 sts

Note: Row 1 is a WS row and is read from left to right.

UNICORN/JAMIESON'S *Chunky Shetland*
(100% wool; 3½oz/100g; 126yds/115m)

Buttons

Accommodate the thickness of the knit fabric when sewing on buttons by making a thread shank. Place a spacer (matchstick, darning needle, or toothpick) across the button and sew over it as you attach the button. Then remove the spacer, bring the needle between the button and fabric, and wrap the yarn around the shank several times before securing with a stitch or two.

65

Teens (and even some adults) can be notoriously difficult to knit garments for, so why not make things easy and knit a backpack? A bulky-weight wool makes the details 'pop' and works up into a sturdy pack in no time. It's loaded with Aran charm and one size does fit all!

Designed by Joan McGowan-Michael

Road-Tested Aran

INTERMEDIATE

7" wide x 7" high x 15" deep

10cm/4"

24

17

•over Broken Rib Pattern

1 2 3 4 **5** 6

• Bulky weight
• 620 yds

• 5mm/US8, or size to obtain gauge, 40cm
(16") long

&

• Cable needle (cn), stitch marker

Broken Rib Pattern *OVER AN ODD NUMBER OF STS*
Worked circularly
Round 1 Knit.
Round 2 * K1, p1; repeat from *, end k1.
Repeat Rounds 1 and 2 for Broken Rib.
Worked back and forth
Row 1 (WS) * P1, k1; repeat from *, end p1.
Row 2 Knit.
Repeat Rows 1 and 2 for Broken Rib.
Notes
1 See *Techniques*, p. 80, for SK2P and
I-cord. **2** Backpack body is worked
circularly, then base is added.

Body
Cast on 120 sts. Place marker, join,
and work circularly. Begin Charts and
Broken Rib Pattern:
Round 1 Work 29 sts in Broken Rib
Pattern, p1, * work 2 sts Chart A, 17 sts
Chart B, 2 sts Chart A, 13 sts Chart C;
repeat from * once more, work 2 sts
Chart A, 17 sts Chart B, 2 sts Chart A, p1.
Continue as established until 20 rounds
of Chart B have been worked 3 times,
then work Rounds 1–8 once more.
Eyelet round K4, yo, k2tog, [k7, yo, k2tog]
2 times, k5, yo, k2tog, k1, p2, yo, p2tog,

p1, k2, p1, yo, p2tog, k2, p2, yo, p2tog,
p1, k2, yo, p2tog, k9, p2tog, yo, k2, p2,
yo, p2tog, p1, k2, p3, k2, p1, yo, p2tog,
p2, k2, yo, p2tog, k9, p2tog, yo, k2, p2,
yo, p2tog, p1, k2, p1, yo, p2tog, k2, p2,
yo, p2tog, p1, k2, p1.
Next round Work Broken Rib Pattern as
established over 29 sts, p1, * k2, p5, k2,
p3, k2, p5, k2, p2, k9, p2; repeat from *
once more, k2, p5, k2, p3, k2, p5, k2, p1.
Repeat last round 3 times more.
Knit 5 rounds.
Next round [K6, MB] 17 times, k1.
Knit 3 rounds.
Bind off. Push last round of bobbles
through to WS.

Base
With RS of body facing, pick up and
knit 29 sts along lower edge of ribbed
section. Work 7" in Broken Rib Pattern
(worked back and forth). Bind off.

Straps (make 2)
Cast on 9 sts. Work 32" in Broken Rib
Pattern (worked back and forth). Bind off.

Finishing

Drawstring

Make one 36" length of 4-st I-cord. Knot ends. Weave cord through eyelets, beginning and ending at eyelets on either side of Chart B cable at center front.

Sew straps on ribbed section on back of body, with top of straps overlapping each other by 2 or 3 sts and placed just below Eyelet round, and with bottom of straps lined up with sides and lower edge of ribbed section (see illustration). Sew 3 sides of Base to Body, easing to fit.

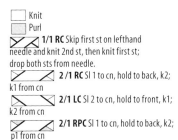

☐ Knit

▨ Purl

1/1 RC Skip first st on lefthand needle and knit 2nd st, then knit first st; drop both sts from needle.

2/1 RC Sl 1 to cn, hold to back, k2; k1 from cn

2/1 LC Sl 2 to cn, hold to front, k1; k2 from cn

2/1 RPC Sl 1 to cn, hold to back, k2; p1 from cn

2/1 LPC Sl 2 to cn, hold to front, p1; k2 from cn

1/3 RC Sl 3 to cn, hold to back, k1; k3 from cn

1/3 LC Sl 1 to cn, hold to front, k3; k1 from cn

B Make Bobble (MB) [K1, yo, k1] in next st, turn, p3; turn, k3; turn, p3; turn, SK2P

BAABAJOES NZ Wool Pak 14-Ply
(100% wool; 9oz/250g; 310yds/283m)

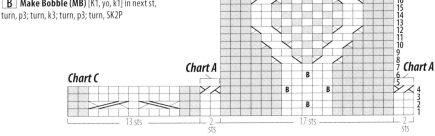

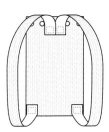

67

You'll be the envy of all your knitting and non-knitting friends with this beautiful counterpane-inspired piece. This is an ideal "take with you everywhere" kind of project. Knit a cotton or linen blend yarn firmly to create a bag that's sure to keep its shape.

Designed by Joan McGowan-Michael

Counterpanes to Go

Notes

1 See *Techniques*, p. 80, for M1, ssk, ssp, and SK2P. *2* Chart is on p. 70-71.

Square (make 4)

Cast on 2 sts. Work 159 rows of Chart. Fasten off last st.

Finishing

With cast-on sts at center, sew all 4 squares together from Rows 1–82, forming a large square.

Linings

Cut 4 pieces from canvas: one 21" × 21" square (bag lining); two 9" × 4½" rectangles (pockets); and one 1¾" × 36" (strap lining). With steam iron, press ½" seam allowances on lining square and pockets.

Note All sewing from this point is done with sewing thread.

Sew pockets to lining, placing them as shown in diagram.

Sew lining to inside of bag, leaving 1" at opposite corners open for strap. Fold corners of bag up as shown and sew squares (including lining) together from Chart rows 83-121.

Strap

Cast on 20 sts and work 36" in St st. Bind off.

Lay lining in strap and fold strap in half lengthwise over lining. Sew edges. Insert ends of strap between lining and bag at open corners and sew securely through all thicknesses. Sew on velcro dots at four points for closures.

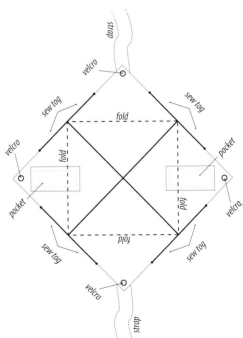

KNITTING FEVER, INC MaggiKnits Linen (52% cotton, 48% linen; 1¾oz/50g; 126yds/114m)

INTERMEDIATE+

13–14" wide x 3½" deep

10cm/4"

30–32
22–24
• over stockinette stitch (knit on RS, purl on WS)

1 2 **3 4** 5 6
•Light–Medium weight
• 840 yds

• 3.5mm/US4, or size to obtain gauge

&

• ²/₃ yd lightweight cotton canvas fabric
• Sewing needle and matching thread
• Two sets velcro dots

68

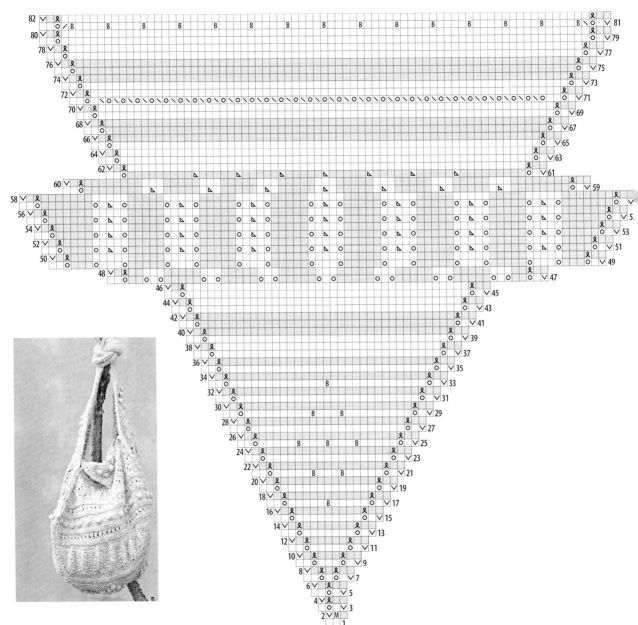

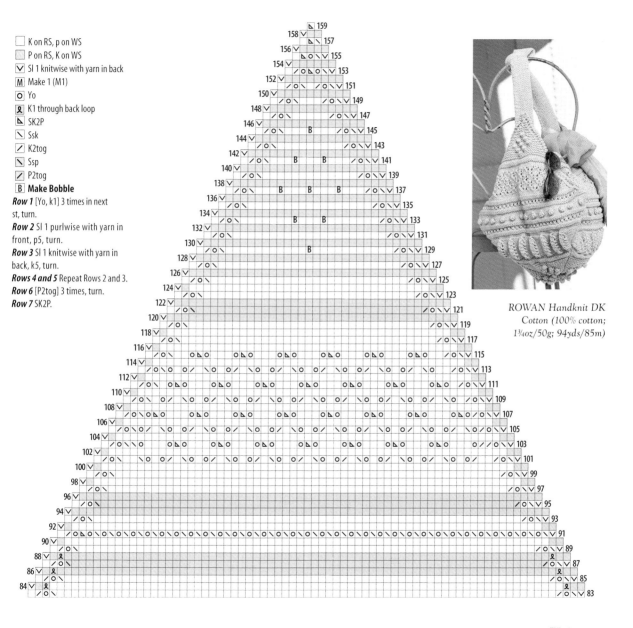

- ☐ K on RS, p on WS
- ▨ P on RS, K on WS
- ☑ Sl 1 knitwise with yarn in back
- Ⓜ Make 1 (M1)
- Ⓞ Yo
- 🅡 K1 through back loop
- ◩ SK2P
- ◲ Ssk
- ☑ K2tog
- ◲ Ssp
- ☑ P2tog
- **Ⓑ Make Bobble**

Row 1 [Yo, k1] 3 times in next
st, turn.
Row 2 Sl 1 purlwise with yarn in
front, p5, turn.
Row 3 Sl 1 knitwise with yarn in
back, k5, turn.
Rows 4 and 5 Repeat Rows 2 and 3.
Row 6 [P2tog] 3 times, turn.
Row 7 SK2P.

ROWAN Handknit DK
Cotton (100% cotton;
1¾oz/50g; 94yds/85m)

71

When a few essentials are all you need, try this treasure pocket. Don't fear metallic yarns (many are easy to knit and block) or beading. The little bag will also be elegant sans beads.

Designed by Nadia Severns

A Treasure of a Pocket

INTERMEDIATE

6¼" wide x 5" high
The bag is made as wide as 2 repeats of the finished lace and about ½" longer than the depth of lace at its longest point.

10cm/4"

48

32

• over stockinette stitch
(knit on RS, purl on WS)

1 **2** 3 4 5 6

• Fine weight
• 208 yds

• 2.25mm/US1, or size to obtain gauge

&

• 2 or 3 small snaps
• Optional beads, see p. 75

Edging
Cast on 19 sts. Work the 30 rows of Mexican Edging 4 times. Bind off. Block lace. On a padded surface, using rust-proof pins, stretch edging to finished size and pin in place. Take care to pin each picot out flat. Do not pierce or split thread while pinning; take care to pin between, not through, stitches. Using a wet press cloth, gently steam lace. Allow to dry thoroughly before unpinning.

Notes
See *Techniques*, p. 80, for cable cast-on, yo, k2tog, and mattress stitch.

BAG
Using cable cast-on, cast on 100 sts. Work even in St st for 5", or until about ½" longer than your blocked lace at its deepest point.

Picot hem
RS row K1, * yo, k2tog; repeat from *, end k1.
Work 5 rows even in St st. Bind off loosely on RS.

Finishing
Pin bag to size and block. When dry, fold in half widthwise, WS together. From RS, with matching yarn and using mattress stitch, sew bottom and side seam of bag. Fold hem to inside along picot row. Steam, then whipstitch in place on WS. Fold lace edging in half, WS together. From RS, invisibly sew side seam. Slip edging, RS up, over bag, placing top of edging just slightly below picot hem at top of bag and matching side seams. Invisibly sew lace to bag by whipstitching through top edge of lace. Sew snaps to inside of bag at base of hem.

Make a twisted cord (see p. 40). Tie a double overhand knot about 2" from each end of cord. Trim ends evenly and allow to unply below knots for tassels. Sew cord in place at sides of bag.

SCHOELLER ESSLINGER *Gold & Silver (80% viscose, 20% lurex; 1oz/25g; 104yds/94m)*

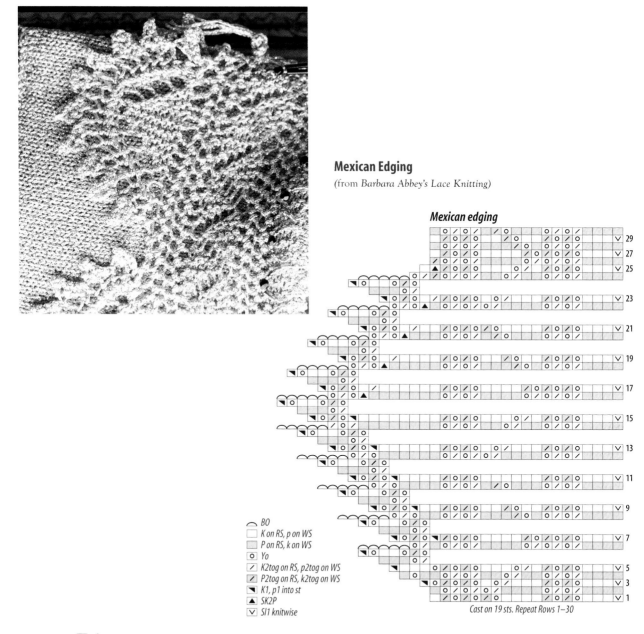

Mexican Edging

(from *Barbara Abbey's Lace Knitting*)

Mexican edging

Legend:
- ⌒ BO
- ☐ K on RS, p on WS
- ▨ P on RS, k on WS
- ⊙ Yo
- ╱ K2tog on RS, p2tog on WS
- ╱ P2tog on RS, k2tog on WS
- ◤ K1, p1 into st
- ▲ SK2P
- ∨ Sl1 knitwise

Cast on 19 sts. Repeat Rows 1–30

Materials

A Assorted glass beads (see Note 1).
B White beading thread, size D or
0. *C* Size 10 English beading needle.
D Small amount beeswax. *E* Fray Check
or clear nail polish.

Notes

1 I used the 'Antique' Japanese cylinder-shaped seed beads called Delicas. They are tubular, have relatively large holes, and come in a wide range of colors, but any size 11 seed bead will work. I used silver-lined gold-colored beads as my base, accented with 2 rosy shades and multi-colored beads with 22K gold lining. The fringe took almost 1 vial of the basic gold color and small amounts of the other colors. I also used 54 antique black 20mm bugle beads, about 70 4mm black, a few 4mm topaz faceted Czech glass beads, and a focus bead.

Beading

After knitting and finishing the treasure bag, fringe along the bottom as follows: Thread your beading needle with an arm's length of beading thread. Wax thread and do not tie a knot. *1* Starting at the lower left-hand corner of the bag, bring threaded needle down from the inside and out the bottom of the bag at the first stitch. Leave a 6" tail to be woven in later. *2* Take a stitch from right to left at the top of the knit stitch to place needle in the correct position (seating stitch). *3* String beads as indicated on fringe

graph for left line of fringe. *4* Skip last (terminal) bead and, holding onto it, bring your needle back up through the entire line of beads just strung. (Do not split the thread with your needle and do not skip a bead up line of fringe. It helps to keep the thread tight and to place the your finger under the line of beads just strung to support them.) *5* When the needle is through all the beads, take another tiny stitch at the top, from right to left. *6* Snake needle along the inside, coming out and down at the next stitch. Repeat from Step 2 along lower edge of bag, reading fringe graph (p. 76) from left to right.

It will be necessary to add new thread several times while working fringe. When about 7" of thread remains, run needle to inside of bag. Knot thread several times around a stitch at base of bag. Seal with a tiny dab of Fray Check or clear nail polish. Clip thread. Begin next thread as you began first. To weave in beginning 6" tails, rethread needle and secure as above.

Top embellishment

I worked 10 swags of fringe across both front and back of bag, seating the stitch and moving across. Bring needle to outside of bag just to the right of strap along top edge of lace. Take a small seating stitch, thread beads (see bead sequence below), skip one picot, bring thread to inside of bag at next picot, and

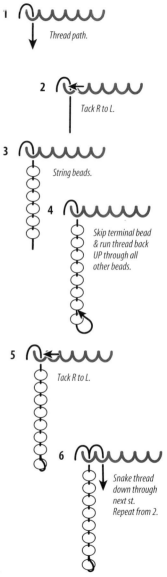

1 *Thread path.*

2 *Tack R to L.*

3 *String beads.*

4 *Skip terminal bead & run thread back UP through all other beads.*

5 *Tack R to L.*

6 *Snake thread down through next st. Repeat from 2.*

75

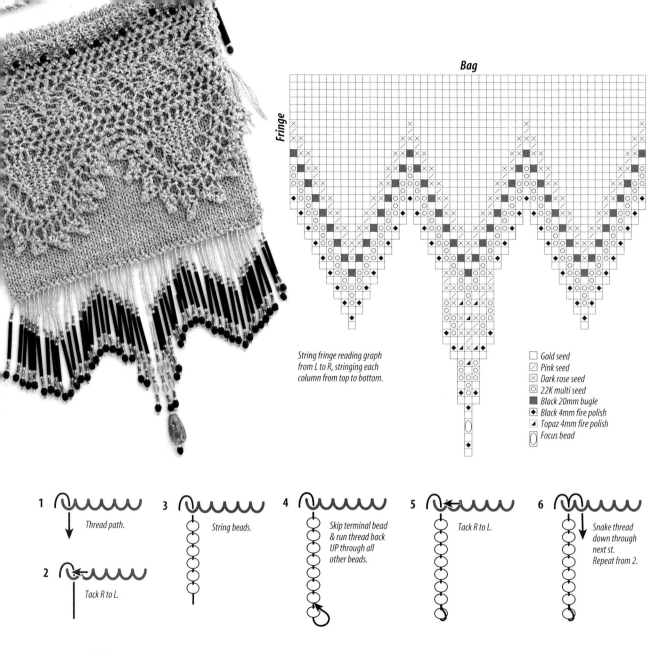

Bag

String fringe reading graph from L to R, stringing each column from top to bottom.

□ Gold seed
▨ Pink seed
⊠ Dark rose seed
◉ 22K multi seed
■ Black 20mm bugle
◆ Black 4mm fire polish
◣ Topaz 4mm fire polish
◯ Focus bead

1 Thread path.

2 Tack R to L.

3 String beads.

4 Skip terminal bead & run thread back UP through all other beads.

5 Tack R to L.

6 Snake thread down through next st. Repeat from 2.

make a small seating stitch to secure. At next picot, make seating stitch, string beads and continue as for first fringe. Repeat across, working a swag at every other picot, for a total of 10 swags. Repeat on other side of bag.

Bead Sequence

Thread beads for each swag as follows: 3 gold, 1 dark rose, 1 pink, 1 dark rose, 3 22K, 1 gold, 1 4mm black, 1 gold, 3 22K, 1 dark rose, 1 pink, 1 dark rose, 3 gold.

Side embellishments

I made small loops of beads around straps at top of bag, stringing beads as follows: 5 gold, 1 dk rose, 1 pink, 1 dk rose, 3 22K, 1 gold, 1 black bugle, 1 gold, 1 4mm black, 1 gold; bring thread around last gold (terminal) bead and back up through 4mm black bead; continue stringing, 1 gold, 1 black bugle, 1 gold, 3 22K, 1 dk rose, 1 pink, 1 dk rose, 5 gold. Secure, then make second loop around other end of strap. Secure beginning 6" tails.

Don't let the small needles and gauge frighten you. The lace is really just ribbing with an occasional cable cross. It is important to knit loosely, so you don't strain your hands and also so that the ribbing is flexible. It takes only an inch or so to get used to the scale of the project.

Designed by Lois Young

Wedding Day Lace

PURSE

Cast on 130 sts. Knit 1 row. Work 8 rows Chart A—108 sts. Work 147 rows Chart B—73 sts. Bind off all sts loosely on WS.

Finishing

Using folding diagram as a guide, block to measurements. Fold with RS together and sew or crochet side seams firmly. Turn right side out.

Line bag as shown. Insert lining in purse; stitch in place. Sew 3 snaps to lining under flap and along front to correspond.

INTERMEDIATE

9½" wide x 4½" high

10cm/4"

56

39

• over stockinette stitch (knit on RS, purl on WS)

 2 3 4 5 6

• Super Fine weight
• 250 yds

• 2mm/US0, or size to obtain gauge

&

• 3 snaps
• 10" x 11½" piece lining
• 10" x 11½" piece interlining

Chart A

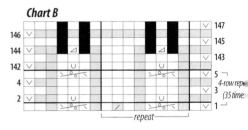

Chart B

Folding diagram

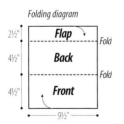

2½" — **Flap** — Fold
4½" — **Back** — Fold
4½" — **Front**
9½"

☐ K on RS, p on WS
▨ P on RS, k on WS
/ P2tog
O Yo
∨ Slip 1 purlwise
⟋ SP2P (sl 1, p2tog, psso)
■ No stitch
Yarnover Cross (YOC) Pull 3rd st over first 2 sts and off needle, then (k1, yo twice, k1) over first 2 sts
U **P Double Cross YO (PDY; WS)** Purl into double yo, dropping 2nd yo
Note Slip sts purlwise with yarn at WS, unless indicated otherwise

DMC Cebelia 10 (100% cotton;
1¾oz/50g; 284yds/258m)
The glove pattern is available
as a free download at
www.knittinguniverse.com

LINING
A beautiful bag deserves a wonderful finish.

knitting

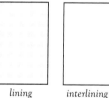

lining

interlining

1 Cut 1 each of lining and interlining (½"
larger than knitting).

2 Place one over
other, RS facing,
and stitch
across bottom.

3 Open and press
along fold lines B & C.

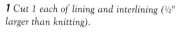

4 Fold, matching
A to C's.

5 Stitch through
all layers, leaving
opening at top.

6 Turn inside out
forming pocket;
stitch opening
closed.

7 Tuck into purse
and stitch in place.

Techniques

Cable cast-on

1 Make a slipknot on left needle

2 Working into this knot's loop, knit a stitch and place it on left needle.

3 Insert right needle between the last 2 stitches. From this position, knit a stitch and place it on left needle.

Repeat Step 3 for each additional stitch.
Or, if adding to existing stitches, hold needle with stitches in left-hand and work Step 3 for each additional stitch.

Techniques index

Crochet cast-on

With crochet hook, chain the number of cast-on stitches required, plus a few extra. With needle and main yarn, beginning at end of chain where stitches were just completed, pick up and knit the exact number of cast-on stitches, picking up stitches in loops at back of chain. Work the piece, usually beginning with a right-side row.

Invisible cast-on

1 Knot working yarn to contrasting waste yarn. With needle in right hand, hold knot in right hand. Tension both strands in left hand; separate the strands with fingers of the left hand. Yarn over with working yarn in front of waste strand.

2 Holding waste strand taut, pivot yarns and yarn over with working yarn in back of waste strand.

3 Each yarn over forms a stitch. Alternate yarn over in front and in back of waste strand for required number of stitches. For an even number, twist working yarn around waste strand before knitting the first row. Later, untie knot, remove waste strand, and arrange bottom loops on needle.

PICK UP AND KNIT

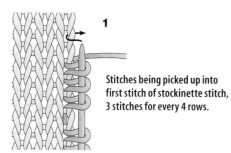

1 Stitches being picked up into first stitch of stockinette stitch, 3 stitches for every 4 rows.

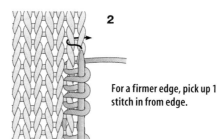

2 For a firmer edge, pick up 1 stitch in from edge.

INCREASES

Make 1 (M1, M1K)

M1L

M1R

For a left-slanting increase (M1L)
With left needle from front of work, pick up strand between last stitch knitted and next stitch. Knit, twisting the strand by working into the loop at the back of the needle.

For a right-slanting increase (M1R)
With left needle from back of work, pick up strand between last stitch knitted and next stitch. Knit, twisting the strand by working into the loop at the front of the needle.

Yarn over (yo)

Before a knit With yarn in front of needle, knit next stitch.

Before a purl With yarn in front of needle, bring yarn over needle and to front again, purl next stitch.

Make 1 purl (M1P)

For a left-slanting increase Work as for M1L, except purl into the loop at the back of the needle.
For a right-slanting increase Work as for M1R, except purl into the loop at the back of the needle.

ABBREVIATIONS

CC contrasting color
cn cable needle
cm centimeter(s)
dec decreas(e)(ed)(es)(ing)
dpn double-pointed needle(s)
g gram(s)
" inch(es)
inc increas(e)(ed)(es)(ing)
k knit(ting)(s)(ted)
LH left-hand
M1 Make one stitch (increase)
m meter(s)
mm millimeter(s)
MC main color
oz ounce(s)
p purl(ed)(ing)(s) or page
pm place marker
psso pass slipped stitch(es) over
RH right-hand
RS right side(s)
rnd round(s)
sc single crochet
sl slip(ped)(ping)
SKP slip, knit, psso
ssk slip, slip, knit these 2 sts tog
ssp slip, slip, purl these 2 sts tog
st(s) stitch(es)
St st stockinette stitch
tbl through back of loop(s)
tog together
WS wrong side(s)
wyib with yarn in back
wyif with yarn in front
yd(s) yard(s)
yo(2) yarn over (twice)

MISCELLANEOUS

Knit through back loop (tbl)

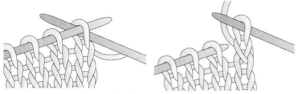

Insert the needle into the stitch from right to left.

I-cord

1 With double-pointed needles, cast on 3 or 4 stitches.
2 Knit. Do not turn work. Slide stitches to opposite end of needle.
Repeat Step 2 until cord is the desired length.

Attached I-cord edging

1 With double-pointed needles, cast on 3 or 4 stitches, then pick up and knit 1 stitch along edge of piece—4 or 5 stitches total.
2 Slide stitches to opposite end of double-pointed needle and k2 or k3, then k2tog through the back loops, pick up and knit 1 stitch from edge.
Repeat Step 2 along edge.

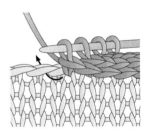

Wrap and turn (W&T) for short rows

Each short row adds 2 rows of knitting across a section of the work. To prevent holes, wrap a stitch at the turn.
On knit row:
1 With yarn in back, slip next stitch as if to purl. Bring yarn to front of work and slip stitch back to left needle as shown. Turn work.
2 When you come to the wrap on the following knit row, knit the wrap together with the stitch it wraps.

Wrap

Hide wrap on next knit row

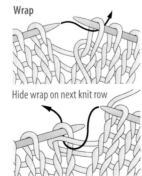

On purl row:
1 With yarn in front, slip next stitch as if to purl. Bring yarn to back of work and slip stitch back to left needle as shown. Turn work.
2 When you come to the wrap on the following purl row, purl the wrap together with the stitch it wraps.

Wrap

Hide wrap on next purl row

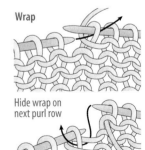

82

Mattress stitch

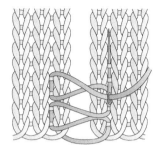

1 After blocking, thread blunt needle with matching yarn.
2 Working with right sides facing, pick up 2 bars between edge stitch and next stitch.
3 Cross to matching place in opposite piece, and pick up 2 bars.
4 Return to first piece, go down into the hole you came out of, and pick up 2 bars.
5 Return to opposite piece, go down into the hole you came out of, and pick up 2 bars.
Repeat Steps 4 and 5 across, pulling thread very tight, then stretching the seam slightly.

Grafting open stitches to bound-off or cast-on edge

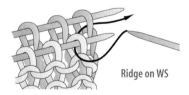

When grafting open stitches to bound-off or cast-on edge, match stitch for stitch.

Grafting stockinette

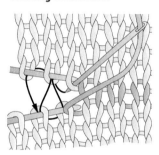

1 Arrange stitches on 2 needles.
2 Thread a blunt needle with matching yarn (approximately 1" per stitch).
3 Working from right to left, with right sides facing you, begin with Steps 3a and 3b:
3a Front needle: yarn through 1st stitch as if to purl, leave stitch on needle.
3b Back needle: yarn through 1st stitch as if to knit, leave on.
4 Work 4a and 4b across:
4a Front needle: through 1st stitch as if to knit, slip off needle; through next st as if to purl, leave on needle.
4b Back needle: through 1st stitch as if to purl, slip off needle; through next st as if to knit, leave on needle.
5 Adjust tension to match rest of knitting.

BIND-OFFS

3-needle bind-off

For bind-off ridge on RS

1 With stitches on 2 needles, place wrong sides together and right side facing you. * K2tog (1 from front needle and 1 from back needle); repeat from * once.

2 Pass first stitch on right needle over 2nd stitch. Continue to k2tog (1 front stitch and 1 back stitch) and bind off across.

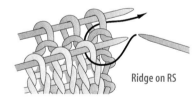

Ridge on RS

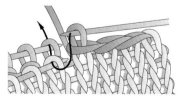

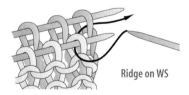

Ridge on WS

For bind-off ridge on WS

Work Steps 1 and 2 but with right sides together and wrong side facing.

DECREASES

ssk

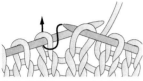

1 Slip 2 stitches separately to right needle as if to knit.

2 Knit these 2 stitches together by slipping left needle into them from left to right.

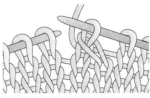

Completed: 2 stitches become one.

sssk

Work same as ssk except:
1 Slip 3 stitches separately to right needle as if to knit.
2 Knit these 3 stitches together by slipping left needle into them from left to right; 3 stitches become one.

S2KP2, SSKP, sl2-k1-p2sso

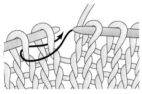

1 Slip 2 stitches together to right needle as if to knit.

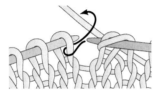

2 Knit next stitch.

3 Pass 2 slipped stitches over knit stitch and off right needle.

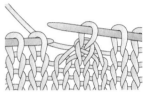

4 Completed: 3 stitches become 1; the center stitch is on top.

ssp

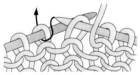

1 Slip 2 stitches separately to right needle as if to knit.

2 Slip these 2 stitches back onto left needle. Insert right needle through their 'back' loops, into the second stitch and then the first.

3 Purl them together.

P2tog

Purl 2 stitches together; 2 stitches become one.

Sk2p, sl1-k2tog-psso

1 Slip one stitch knitwise.
2 Knit next two stitches together.
3 Pass the slipped stitch over the k2tog.

84

S2PP2

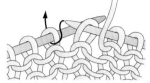 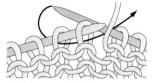  

1 Slip 2 stitches separately to right needle as if to knit.

2 Slip these 2 stitches back onto left needle. Insert right needle through their 'back loops,' into the second stitch and then the first and slip 2 stitches to right needle.

3 Purl next stitch.

4 Pass 2 slipped stitches over purl stitch and off right needle; the center stitch is on top.

CROCHET

Single crochet (SC) Work slip stitch to begin.

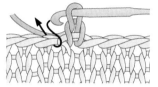  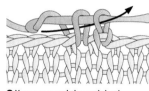

1 Insert hook into next stitch.

2 Yarn over and through stitch; 2 loops on hook.

3 Yarn over and through both loops on hook; single crochet completed. Repeat Steps 1–3.

Crochet chain

Make a slipknot to begin.
1 Yarn over hook, draw yarn through loop on hook.

2 First chain made. Repeat Step 1.

Backwards single crochet

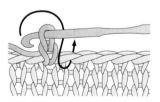 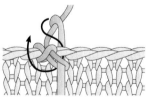 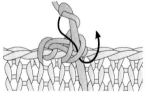 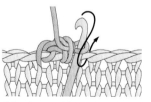

1 Work from left to right.
1a Work a slip stitch to begin.
1b Insert hook into next stitch to right.

2 Bring yarn through stitch only. As soon as hook clears the stitch, flip your wrist (and the hook). There are now 2 loops on the hook, and the just-made loop is to the front of the hook (left of the old loop).

3 Yarn over and through both loops on hook; one backwards single crochet completed.

4 Continue working to right, repeating from Step 1b.

85

Specifications:

INTERMEDIATE
One size
20" circumference x 9" deep

10cm/4"

27

21

over stockinette stitch
(k on RS, p on WS)

1 2 3 **4** 5 6

Medium weight
MC, A, B, C, D, E, F • 88yds each

Four 4.5mm/US7 double-pointed needles
(dpn) or size to obtain gauge

4.5mm/US7 circular 40cm (16") long

&

Stitch marker, yarn needle

Skill level
Size

Gauge
*The number of stitches and
rows you need in 10 cm or
4", worked as specified.*

Yarn weight
and amount in yards

Type of needles
*Straight, unless circular or
double-pointed
are recommended.*

Any extras

Conversion chart

centimeters	0.394	inches
grams	0.035	ounces
inches	2.54	centimeters
ounces	28.6	grams
meters	1.1	yards
yards	.91	meters

Needles/Hooks

US	MM	HOOK
0	2	A
1	2.25	B
2	2.75	C
3	3.25	D
4	3.5	E
5	3.75	F
6	4	G
7	4.5	7
8	5	H
9	5.5	I
10	6	J
10½	6.5	K
11	8	L
13	9	M
15	10	N
17	12.75	

At a Glance

Yarn weight categories

Yarn Weight

1	**2**	**3**	**4**	**5**	**6**
Super Fine	**Fine**	**Light**	**Medium**	**Bulky**	**Super Bulky**

Also called

Sock	Sport	DK	Worsted	Chunky	Bulky
Fingering	Baby	Light-	Afghan	Craft	Roving
Baby		Worsted	Aran	Rug	

Stockinette Stitch Gauge Range 10cm/4 inches

27 sts	23 sts	21 sts	16 sts	12 sts	6 sts
to	to	to	to	to	to
32 sts	26 sts	24 sts	20 sts	15 sts	11 sts

Recommended needle (metric)

2.25 mm	3.25 mm	3.75 mm	4.5 mm	5.5 mm	8 mm
to	to	to	to	to	and
3.25 mm	3.75 mm	4.5 mm	5.5 mm	8 mm	larger

Recommended needle (US)

1 to 3	3 to 5	5 to 7	7 to 9	9 to 11	11 and larger

Locate the Yarn Weight and Stockinette Stitch Gauge Range over 10cm to 4" on the chart. Compare that range with the information on the yarn label to find an appropriate yarn. These are guidelines only for commonly used gauges and needle sizes in specific yarn categories.

Equivalent weights

¾	oz		20 g
1	oz		28 g
1½	oz		40 g
1¾	oz		50 g
2	oz		60 g
3½	oz		100 g

More on the way...

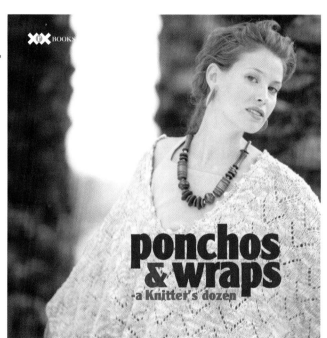

Contributors

Lynda Cyr

Jane Davis

Chris de Longpre

Edie Eckman

Bev Galeskas

Cynthia Helene

Lori Ihnen

Laura Kochevar

Megan Lacey

Ginger Luters

Susanna Lewis

Joan McGowan-Michael

Shanta Moitra

Nadia Severns

Lois Young